Collins

Italian

Vocabulary

HarperCollins Publishers
Westerhill Road
Bishopbriggs
Glasgow
G64 2QT
Great Britain

Second Edition 2012

Reprint 10 9 8 7 6 5 4 3 2 1 0

ISBN 978-0-00-748394-5

www.collinslanguage.com

A catalogue record for this book is available from the British Library

Typeset by Davidson Publishing Solutions, Glasgow

Printed in Great Britain by Clays Ltd, St Ives plc

Acknowledgements
We would like to thank those authors and publishers who kindly gave permission for copyright material to be used in the Collins Word Web. We would also like to thank Times Newspapers Ltd for providing valuable data.

EDITOR
Persephone Lock

CONTRIBUTORS
Phyllis Buchanan
Gabriella Bacchelli
Federico Bonfanti

FOR THE PUBLISHER
Lucy Cooper
Elaine Higgleton
Susanne Reichert
Lisa Sutherland

William Collins' dream of knowledge for all began with the publication of his first book in 1819. A self-educated mill worker, he not only enriched millions of lives, but also founded a flourishing publishing house. Today, staying true to this spirit, Collins books are packed with inspiration, innovation, and practical expertise. They place you at the centre of a world of possibility and give you exactly what you need to explore it.

Language is the key to this exploration, and at the heart of Collins Dictionaries is language as it is really used. New words, phrases, and meanings spring up every day, and all of them are captured and analysed by the Collins Word Web. Constantly updated, and with over 4.5 billion entries, this living language resource is unique to our dictionaries.

Words are tools for life. And a Collins Dictionary makes them work for you.

Collins. Do more.

 contents

The *Easy Learning Italian Vocabulary* is designed for both young and adult learners. Whether you are starting to learn Italian for the first time, revising for school exams or simply want to brush up on your Italian, the *Easy Learning Italian Vocabulary* offers you the information you require in a clear and accessible format.

This book is divided into 50 topics, arranged in alphabetical order. This thematic approach enables you to learn related words and phrases together, so that you can become confident in using particular vocabulary in context.

Vocabulary within each topic is divided into nouns and useful phrases which are aimed at helping you to express yourself in idiomatic Italian. Vocabulary within each topic is graded to help you prioritize your learning. Essential words include the basic words you will need to be able to communicate effectively, important words help expand your knowledge, and useful words provide additional vocabulary which will enable you to express yourself more fully.

Nouns are grouped by gender: masculine ("il") nouns are given on the left-hand page, and feminine ("la") nouns on the right-hand page, enabling you to memorize words according to their gender. In addition, all feminine forms of adjectives are shown, as are irregular, invariable and gender-changing noun plurals.

At the end of the book you will find a list of supplementary vocabulary, grouped according to part of speech – adjective, verb, noun and so on. This is vocabulary which you will come across in many everyday situations.

Finally, there is an English index which lists all the essential and important nouns given under the topic headings for quick reference.

The *Easy Learning Italian Vocabulary* helps you to consolidate your language learning. Together with the other titles in the *Easy Learning* range you can be sure that you have all the help you need when learning Italian at your fingertips.

ABBREVIATIONS

adj	adjective
adv	adverb
conj	conjunction
f	feminine
inv	invariable
m	masculine
m+f	masculine and feminine form
n	noun
pl	plural
pl inv	invariable, with no change to noun in the plural
prep	preposition
qc	qualcosa
qn	qualcuno
sb	somebody
sing	singular
sth	something

The swung dash ~ is used to indicate no change to a word in the plural of a compound noun.

GENDER

In Italian, nouns are either masculine or feminine. Most masculine nouns take the article il. This article becomes l' when the noun begins with a vowel and becomes lo when the noun begins with s+consonant (eg sc, sp, st), or begins gn, pn, ps, x, y or z.
Feminine nouns take la or l' (when the noun begins with a vowel).

Many masculine nouns end in o; many feminine nouns end in a. Both masculine and feminine nouns can end in e.

PLURAL

Unlike English, where you generally add letters (s or es) to make nouns plural, in Italian you change the final letter.
o > **i** (il post**o** > i post**i**)
a > **e** (la pizz**a** > le pizz**e**)
e > **i** (il padr**e**, la madr**e** > i padr**i**, le madr**i**)
Articles change as follows:

masculine:	il > i	l' > gli	lo > gli
feminine:	la > le	l' > le	

Nouns that are imported into Italian (such as bar, computer, menù, sport) stay the same in the plural (*pl inv*). They are generally masculine:
il bar > i bar, il computer > i computer, il menù > i menù, lo sport > gli sport.

PLURAL SPELLING CHANGES

Most nouns ending -co, -ca, -go and -ga often require an h inserting in the plural to retain the hard 'kuh' and 'guh' sounds:
il parco > i parchi, la banca > le banche
il lago > i laghi, la targa > le targhe
Where spelling changes occur in the plural we have included the plural ending.

air travel

ESSENTIAL WORDS *(masculine)*

un **aereo**	plane
un **aeroplano**	aeroplane
un **aeroporto**	airport
un **agente di viaggio**	travel agent
l' **arrivo**	arrival
il **bagaglio**	luggage
il **bagaglio a mano**	hand luggage
il **banco**	desk
il **biglietto**	ticket
il **carrello**	trolley
il **check-in**	check in
il **doganiere**	customs officer
l' **imbarco**	boarding
il **noleggio auto**	car hire
il **numero**	number
un **orario**	timetable
il **passaporto**	passport
il **passeggero**	passenger
il **prezzo del biglietto**	fare
il **ritardo**	delay
il **taxi** *(pl inv)*	taxi
il **turista**	tourist; holiday maker
il **viaggiatore**	traveller
il **viaggio**	trip
il **volo**	flight

USEFUL PHRASES

viaggiare in aereo to travel by plane
un biglietto di sola andata a one-way ticket
un biglietto di andata e ritorno a return ticket
prenotare un biglietto aereo to book a plane ticket
fare il check-in del bagaglio to check in luggage
l'aereo è decollato/atterrato the plane has taken off/landed
il tabellone degli arrivi/delle partenze the arrivals/departures board
il volo numero 776 proveniente da Roma/diretto a Roma flight number 776 from Rome/to Rome

ESSENTIAL WORDS *(feminine)*

un'	**agente di viaggio**	travel agent
la	**borsa**	bag
la	**cancellazione**	cancellation
la	**carta d'identità**	ID card
la	**carta d'imbarco**	boarding card
la	**coincidenza**	connection
la	**dogana**	customs
la	**doganiera**	customs officer
l'	**entrata**	entrance
le	**informazioni**	information desk; information
la	**partenza**	departure
la	**passeggera**	passenger
la	**prenotazione**	reservation
la	**tariffa**	fare
le	**toilette**	toilets
la	**turista**	tourist; holiday maker
l'	**uscita**	exit; gate
l'	**uscita d'emergenza**	emergency exit
l'	**uscita d'imbarco**	departure gate
la	**valigia**	bag; suitcase
la	**viaggiatrice**	traveller

USEFUL PHRASES

ho perso la coincidenza I missed my connection
ritirare la valigia to collect one's luggage
"ritiro bagagli" "baggage reclaim"
passare per la dogana to go through customs
ho qualcosa da dichiarare I have something to declare
non ho niente da dichiarare I have nothing to declare
controllare il bagaglio to search the luggage
voli nazionali/internazionali domestic/international flights

air travel

IMPORTANT WORDS *(masculine)*

il	**biglietto elettronico**	e-ticket
il	**corridoio**	aisle
un	**elicottero**	helicopter
il	**finestrino**	window
un	**incidente aereo**	plane crash
il	**mal d'aria**	airsickness
il	**pilota**	pilot

USEFUL WORDS *(masculine)*

un	**assistente di volo**	flight attendant
un	**atterraggio**	landing
i	**comandi**	controls
il	**controllo di sicurezza**	security check
il	**controllore del traffico aereo**	air-traffic controller
il	**decollo**	take-off
i	**diritti di dogana**	customs duty
un	**equipaggio**	crew
l'	**imbarco** *(pl* **-chi***)*	boarding
il	**jumbo** *(pl inv)*	jumbo jet
il	**metal detector** *(pl inv)*	metal detector
il	**nastro trasportatore**	carousel
un	**orario**	timetable
il	**paracadute** *(pl inv)*	parachute
il	**posto (a sedere)**	seat
il	**radar** *(pl inv)*	radar
il	**reattore**	jet engine
lo	**scalo**	stopover
lo	**steward** *(pl inv)*	steward
il	**terminal** *(pl inv)*	terminal
il	**vuoto d'aria**	air pocket

USEFUL PHRASES

a bordo on board; **"vietato fumare"** "no smoking"
in ritardo delayed; **in orario** on time
"allacciare le cinture di sicurezza" "fasten your seat belts"
stiamo volando sopra Londra we are flying over London
ho la nausea I am feeling sick; **fare un dirottamento aereo** to hijack a plane

IMPORTANT WORDS *(feminine)*

la	**cintura di sicurezza**	seat belt
la	**durata**	length; duration
la	**mappa**	map
la	**sala d'imbarco**	departure lounge
la	**velocità** *(pl inv)*	speed

USEFUL WORDS *(feminine)*

un'	**ala**	wing
l'	**altezza**	height
l'	**altitudine**	altitude
un'	**assistente di volo**	flight attendant
la	**barriera del suono**	sound barrier
un'	**elica** *(pl* **-che***)*	propeller
un'	**etichetta**	label
la	**hostess** *(pl inv)*	air hostess
la	**linea aerea**	airline
la	**pista (d'atterraggio)**	runway
la	**rivista**	magazine
la	**scala mobile**	escalator
la	**scatola nera**	black box
la	**torre di controllo**	control tower
la	**turbolenza**	turbulence

USEFUL PHRASES

"i passeggeri del volo AB251 con destinazione Roma sono pregati di procedere all'imbarco all'uscita 51" "flight AB251 to Rome now boarding at gate 51"

abbiamo fatto scalo a New York we stopped over in New York

un atterraggio d'emergenza an emergency landing

un atterraggio di fortuna a crash landing

animals

ESSENTIAL WORDS *(masculine)*

un **agnello**	lamb
un **animale**	animal
il **bue** *(pl* **buoi**)	ox
il **cane**	dog
il **cavallo**	horse
il **cinghiale**	wild boar
il **coniglio**	rabbit
il **criceto**	hamster
il **cucciolo**	puppy
un **elefante**	elephant
il **gattino**	kitten
il **gatto**	cat
il **giardino zoologico**	zoo
il **leone**	lion
il **maiale**	pig
il **pelo**	coat, hair
il **pesce**	fish
il **topo**	mouse
un **uccello**	bird
il **vitello**	calf
il **volpe**	fox
lo **zoo** *(pl inv)*	zoo

USEFUL PHRASES

mi piacciono i gatti, odio i serpenti, preferisco i cani I like cats, I hate snakes, I prefer dogs

in casa abbiamo 12 animali we have 12 pets in our house

non abbiamo animali in casa we have no pets in our house

gli animali selvatici wild animals

gli animali domestici pets

il bestiame livestock

mettere un animale in gabbia to put an animal in a cage

liberare un animale to set an animal free

ESSENTIAL WORDS *(feminine)*

la **cagna**	dog *(female)*
la **gatta**	cat *(female)*
la **mucca** *(pl* **-che***)*	cow
la **pecora**	ewe
la **pelliccia** *(pl* **-ce***)*	fur
la **scimmia**	monkey
la **tartaruga** *(pl* **-ghe***)*	tortoise
la **tigre**	tiger

IMPORTANT WORDS *(feminine)*

la **caccia**	hunting
la **coda**	tail
la **gabbia**	cage
la **zampa**	paw

USEFUL PHRASES

il cane abbaia the dog barks; **ringhia** it growls
il gatto miagola the cat miaows; **fa le fusa** it purrs
mi piace l'equitazione *or* **andare a cavallo** I like horse-riding
a cavallo on horseback
"attenti al cane" "beware of the dog"
"è vieteto introdurre cani" "no dogs allowed"
"a cuccia!" *(to dog)* "down!"
i diritti degli animali animal rights
andare a caccia to go hunting

animals

USEFUL WORDS *(masculine)*

un	**artiglio**	claw *(of lion, tiger)*
un	**asino**	donkey
il	**cammello**	camel
il	**canguro**	kangaroo
il	**canile**	kennel
il	**caprone**	billy goat
il	**carapace**	shell *(of tortoise)*
il	**cervo**	deer, stag
il	**coccodrillo**	crocodile
il	**corno**	horn
il	**guinzaglio**	dog lead
un	**ippopotamo**	hippopotamus
il	**lupo**	wolf
il	**maiale**	pig
il	**marsupio**	pouch *(of kangaroo)*
il	**mulo**	mule
il	**muso**	muzzle; snout
il	**negozio di animali**	pet shop
un	**orso**	bear
un	**orso polare**	polar bear
il	**pipistrello**	bat
il	**pony** *(pl inv)*	pony
il	**porcellino d'india**	guinea pig
il	**puledro**	foal
il	**ratto**	rat
il	**riccio**	hedgehog
il	**rinoceronte**	rhinoceros
il	**rospo**	toad
lo	**scoiattolo**	squirrel
il	**serpente**	snake
lo	**squalo**	shark
il	**toro**	bull
lo	**zoccolo**	hoof

USEFUL WORDS *(feminine)*

la **balena**	whale
la **biscia** *(pl* **-sce***)*	snake
la **bocca** *(pl* **-che***)*	mouth
la **capra**	(nanny) goat
la **cavalla**	mare
la **cavia**	guinea pig
la **cerva**	doe
le **corna**	antlers; horns
la **criniera**	mane
la **foca** *(pl* **-che***)*	seal
la **giraffa**	giraffe
la **gobba**	hump *(of camel)*
la **leonessa**	lioness
la **lepre**	hare
la **lucertola**	lizard
la **mula**	mule
la **pelle**	hide *(of cow, elephant etc)*
la **proboscide**	trunk *(of elephant)*
la **rana**	frog
le **strisce**	stripes *(of zebra)*
la **talpa**	mole
la **tigre**	tigress
la **trappola**	trap
la **vipera**	viper; adder
la **volpe**	fox
la **zanna**	tusk
la **zebra**	zebra

bikes

ESSENTIAL WORDS *(masculine)*

il **casco** *(pl* **-chi***)*	helmet
il **ciclismo**	cycling
il **ciclista**	cyclist
il **fanale**	lamp
il **freno**	brake

IMPORTANT WORDS *(masculine)*

il **pedale**	pedal
il **sellino**	saddle

USEFUL WORDS *(masculine)*

il **cambio**	derailleur; gears
il **campanello**	bell
il **catarifrangente**	reflector
il **cestino**	pannier
il **Giro d'Italia**	Tour of Italy
il **kit** *(pl inv)* **per riparare le gomme**	puncture repair kit
il **lucchetto**	padlock
il **manubrio**	handlebars
il **mozzo**	hub
il **parafango** *(pl* **-ghi***)*	mudguard
il **portapacchi** *(pl inv)*	carrier
il **raggio**	spoke
il **telaio**	frame
il **tubolare**	tyre

USEFUL PHRASES

andare in bici(cletta) to go by bike, to cycle
sono venuto in bici(cletta) I came by bike
pedalare to pedal
a tutta velocità at full speed
cambiare marcia to change gear
fermarsi to stop
frenare bruscamente to brake suddenly

ESSENTIAL WORDS *(feminine)*

la	**bici** *(pl inv)*	bike
la	**bicicletta**	bicycle
la	**ciclista**	cyclist
la	**city bike** *(pl inv)*	city bike
la	**mountain bike** *(pl inv)*	mountain bike
la	**sella**	saddle

IMPORTANT WORDS *(feminine)*

la	**camera d'aria**	inner tube
la	**discesa**	descent
la	**foratura**	puncture
la	**gomma**	tyre
la	**marcia** *(pl* **-ce***)*	gear
la	**pista ciclabile**	cycle lane
la	**pompa**	pump
la	**ruota**	wheel
la	**salita**	climb
la	**velocità** *(pl inv)*	speed

USEFUL WORDS *(feminine)*

la	**caduta**	fall
la	**canna superiore**	crossbar
la	**catena**	chain
la	**cima**	top *(of hill)*
la	**dinamo** *(pl inv)*	dynamo
la	**luce anteriore**	front light
la	**valvola**	valve

USEFUL PHRASES

fare un giro in bici(cletta) to go for a bike ride
bucare to have a puncture
riparare una gomma to mend a puncture
la ruota anteriore/posteriore the front/back wheel
gonfiare le ruote to blow up the tyres
lucido(a) shiny
fluorescente fluorescent

birds

ESSENTIAL WORDS *(masculine)*

il	**cielo**	sky
il	**gallo**	cock
il	**pappagallino**	budgie
il	**pappagallo**	parrot
il	**tacchino**	turkey
un	**uccello**	bird

USEFUL WORDS *(masculine)*

un	**avvoltoio**	vulture
il	**becco** *(pl* **-chi***)*	beak
il	**canarino**	canary
il	**cigno**	swan
il	**corvo**	raven
il	**cuculo**	cuckoo
il	**fagiano**	pheasant
il	**falcone**	falcon
il	**gabbiano**	seagull
il	**gallo cedrone**	grouse
il	**gufo**	owl
il	**martin pescatore**	kingfisher
il	**merlo**	blackbird
il	**nido**	nest
il	**passero**	sparrow
il	**pavone**	peacock
il	**pettirosso**	robin
il	**picchio**	woodpecker
il	**piccione**	pigeon
il	**pinguino**	penguin
lo	**scricciolo**	wren
lo	**storno**	starling
lo	**struzzo**	ostrich
il	**tordo**	thrush
un	**uccello rapace**	bird of prey
un	**uovo** *(pl f* **uova***)*	egg
un	**usignolo**	nightingale

ESSENTIAL WORDS *(feminine)*

un'	**ala**	wing
un'	**anatra**	duck
la	**gallina**	hen
un'	**oca** (*pl* **-che**)	goose

USEFUL WORDS *(feminine)*

un'	**allodola**	lark
un'	**aquila**	eagle
la	**cicogna**	stork
la	**cinciarella**	bluetit
la	**colomba**	dove
la	**gabbia**	cage
l'	**Influenza avaria**	bird flu
la	**gazza**	magpie
la	**pernice**	partridge
la	**piuma**	feather
la	**quaglia**	quail
la	**rondine**	swallow
la	**taccola**	jackdaw
le	**uova**	eggs

USEFUL PHRASES

volare to fly
volare via to fly away
costruire un nido to build a nest
fischiare to whistle
cantare to sing
la gente li mette in gabbia people put them in cages
covare un uovo to sit on an egg
un uccello migratore a migratory bird

body

ESSENTIAL WORDS *(masculine)*

il	**braccio** *(pl f* **braccia***)*	arm
i	**capelli**	hair
il	**corpo**	body
il	**cuore**	heart
il	**dente**	tooth
il	**dito** *(pl f* **dita***)*	finger
il	**ginocchio**	knee
il	**naso**	nose
un	**occhio**	eye
un	**orecchio** *(pl f* **orecchie***)*	ear
il	**pelo**	hair
il	**piede**	foot
lo	**stomaco**	stomach
il	**viso**	face

IMPORTANT WORDS *(masculine)*

il	**collo**	neck
il	**mento**	chin
il	**petto**	chest; bust
il	**pollice**	thumb
il	**sangue**	blood
il	**sopracciglio** *(pl f* **sopracciglia***)*	eyebrow

USEFUL PHRASES

in piedi standing
seduto(a) sitting
disteso(a) lying

ESSENTIAL WORDS *(feminine)*

la **bocca** *(pl* **-che***)*	mouth
le **braccia**	arms
le **dita**	fingers
la **gamba**	leg
la **gola**	throat
la **mano** *(pl* **mani***)*	hand
la **narice**	nostril
la **schiena**	back
la **testa**	head

IMPORTANT WORDS *(feminine)*

la **caviglia**	ankle
la **faccia** *(pl* **-ce***)*	face
la **fronte**	forehead
la **guancia** *(pl* **-ce***)*	cheek
la **lingua**	tongue
le **orecchie**	ears
la **pelle**	skin
le **sopracciglia**	eyebrows
la **spalla**	shoulder
la **voce**	voice

USEFUL PHRASES

grande big
alto(a) tall
piccolo(a) small
basso(a) short
grasso(a) fat
magro(a) skinny
snello(a) slim
bello(a) beautiful; handsome
carino(a) pretty; cute
brutto(a) ugly

USEFUL WORDS *(masculine)*

il	**cervello**	brain
il	**ciglio** *(pl f* **ciglia***)*	eyelash
il	**dito del piede**	toe
il	**ditone**	the big toe
il	**fegato**	liver
il	**fianco**	hip
il	**gesto**	gesture
il	**gomito**	elbow
un	**indice**	forefinger
il	**labbro** *(pl f* **labbra***)*	lip
i	**lineamenti**	features
il	**muscolo**	muscle
un	**osso** *(pl f* **ossa***)*	bone
il	**polmone**	lung
il	**polpaccio**	calf *(of leg)*
il	**polso**	wrist
il	**pugno**	fist
il	**rene**	kidney
lo	**scheletro**	skeleton
il	**sedere**	bottom
il	**seno**	breast
il	**tallone**	heel
il	**tratto**	feature

USEFUL PHRASES

soffiarsi il naso to blow one's nose
tagliarsi le unghie to cut one's nails
tagliarsi i capelli to have one's hair cut
scrollare le spalle to shrug one's shoulders
fare cenno di sì con il capo to nod one's head *(say yes)*
fare cenno di no con il capo to shake one's head *(say no)*
vedere to see; **sentire** to hear; to feel
annusare to smell; **toccare** to touch; **assaggiare** to taste
stringere la mano a qn to shake hands with sb
salutare qn con la mano to wave at sb
indicare qc to point at sth

USEFUL WORDS *(feminine)*

un'	**anca** *(pl* **-che***)*	hip
un'	**arteria**	artery
la	**carnagione**	skin, complexion
la	**carne**	flesh
le	**ciglia**	eyelashes
la	**colonna vertebrale**	spine
la	**coscia** *(pl* **-sce***)*	thigh
la	**costola**	rib
le	**dita del piede**	toes
la	**fronte**	temple *(of head)*
le	**labbra**	lips
la	**mandibola**	jaw
la	**nuca** *(pl* **-che***)*	nape of the neck
le	**ossa**	bones
la	**palpebra**	eyelid
la	**pianta del piede**	sole of the foot
la	**pupilla**	pupil *(of the eye)*
la	**taglia**	size
un'	**unghia**	nail
la	**vena**	vein
la	**vita**	waist

USEFUL PHRASES

(misura dei) fianchi hip measurement
giro vita waist measurement
(misura del) petto chest measurement
sordo(a) deaf
cieco(a) blind
muto(a) mute
disabile disabled
persona con difficoltà d'apprendimento person with learning difficulties
lui è più alto di te he is taller than you
Sara è cresciuta molto Sara has grown a lot
sono in sovrappeso I am overweight
è ingrassata/dimagrita she has put on weight/lost weight
è alta 1 metro e 47 she is 1.47 metres tall
pesa 40 chili he/she weighs 40 kilos

SEASONS

la **primavera**	spring
l' **estate** *(f)*	summer
l' **autunno** *(m)*	autumn
l' **inverno** *(m)*	winter

MONTHS

gennaio	January
febbraio	February
marzo	March
aprile	April
maggio	May
giugno	June
luglio	July
agosto	August
settembre	September
ottobre	October
novembre	November
dicembre	December

DAYS OF THE WEEK

lunedì	Monday
martedì	Tuesday
mercoledì	Wednesday
giovedì	Thursday
venerdì	Friday
sabato	Saturday
domenica	Sunday

USEFUL PHRASES

in primavera/estate/autunno/inverno in spring/summer/autumn/winter
in maggio in May
il 10 luglio 2009 on 10 July 2009
è il 3 dicembre it's 3rd December
di sabato vado in piscina on Saturdays I go to the swimming pool
sabato sono andato in piscina on Saturday I went to the swimming pool
il prossimo sabato/sabato scorso next/last Saturday
il sabato prima/dopo the previous/following Saturday

un	**anno**	year
il	**calendario**	calendar
i	**giorni della settimana**	days of the week
il	**giorno**	day
il	**giorno festivo**	public holiday
il	**mese**	month
la	**settimana**	week
la	**stagione**	season

USEFUL PHRASES

fare ponte to take a long weekend
il primo aprile the first of April, April Fools' Day
il pesce d'aprile April Fools' trick
il primo maggio Labour day
il carnevale carnival period prior to Lent
l'Epifania Epiphany (6 January)
Ferragosto August 15 (Bank Holiday in Italy)
San Valentino St Valentine's Day
Ognissanti All Saints' Day
Pasqua Easter
Domenica di Pasqua Easter Sunday
Pasquetta or **Lunedì di Pasqua** Easter Monday
Mercoledì delle Ceneri Ash Wednesday
Venerdì Santo Good Friday
la Quaresima Lent
la Pasqua ebraica Passover
il Ramadan Ramadan
Hanukkah Hanukkah *or* Hanukah
la vigilia di Natale Christmas Eve
Natale Christmas
il giorno di Natale Christmas Day
San Silvestro New Year's Eve
Capodanno New Year's Day; New Year's Eve
il cenone/festa di Capodanno New Year's Eve dinner/party

ESSENTIAL WORDS *(masculine)*

un	**anniversario di matrimonio**	wedding anniversary
un	**appuntamento**	appointment, date
il	**biglietto d'auguri**	greetings card
il	**compleanno**	birthday
il	**divorzio**	divorce
il	**matrimonio**	marriage; wedding
un	**onomastico**	saint's day
il	**regalo**	present

IMPORTANT WORDS *(masculine)*

il	**falò** *(pl inv)*	bonfire
il	**fidanzamento**	engagement
i	**fuochi d'artificio**	fireworks; firework display
il	**parco** *(pl* **-chi***)* **dei divertimenti**	fun fair

USEFUL WORDS *(masculine)*

il	**battesimo**	christening
il	**cimitero**	cemetery
il	**funerale**	funeral
il	**regalo di Natale**	Christmas present
il	**testimone**	witness

USEFUL PHRASES

festeggiare il compleanno to celebrate one's birthday
mia sorella è nata nel 1995 my sister was born in 1995
ha appena compiuto 17 anni he/she has just turned 17
mi ha fatto un regalo he/she gave me a present
te lo regalo! I'm giving it to you!
grazie thank you
divorziare to get divorced
sposarsi to get married
fidanzarsi (con qn) to get engaged (to sb)
mio padre è morto due anni fa my father died two years ago
seppellire to bury

ESSENTIAL WORDS *(feminine)*

la **data**	date
la **festa**	party; birthday
la **morte**	death
la **nascita**	birth
le **nozze**	wedding

IMPORTANT WORDS *(feminine)*

le **feste**	festivities
la **fiera**	fair
la **sagra**	festival

USEFUL WORDS *(feminine)*

la **cerimonia**	ceremony
la **damigella (d'onore)**	bridesmaid
la **luna di miele**	honeymoon
la **participazione (di nozze)**	wedding invitation
la **pensione**	retirement
la **prima comunione**	first communion
la **processione**	procession
la **testimone**	witness

USEFUL PHRASES

nozze d'oro/argento/diamante silver/golden/diamond wedding anniversary
fare gli auguri di Buon Anno a qn to wish sb a happy New Year
dare una festa to have a party
invitare gli amici to invite friends
scegliere un regalo to choose a gift
Buon Natale! Happy Christmas!
Buon compleanno! happy birthday!
auguri best wishes

camping

ESSENTIAL WORDS *(masculine)*

il	**bidone della spazzatura**	dustbin
il	**campeggiatore**	camper
il	**campeggio**	camping; campsite
il	**camper** *(pl inv)*	camper van
il	**coltello**	knife
il	**cucchiaio**	spoon
il	**fiammifero**	match
il	**gas** *(pl inv)*	gas
il	**piatto**	plate
il	**picchetto**	tent peg
il	**posto**	place; vacancy
i	**servizi**	washrooms; toilets
lo	**specchio**	mirror
il	**supplemento**	extra charge
il	**tavolino**	table
il	**temperino**	penknife
il	**veicolo**	vehicle

IMPORTANT WORDS *(masculine)*

un	**apribottiglie** *(pl inv)*	corkscrew
un	**apriscatole** *(pl inv)*	tin-opener
il	**barbecue** *(pl inv)*	barbecue
il	**bucato**	washing
il	**detersivo**	washing powder
il	**fango** *(pl* **-ghi***)*	mud
il	**fornello**	stove
un	**igloo** *(pl inv)*	dome tent
il	**martello**	hammer
il	**materassino gonfiabile**	airbed
il	**regolamento**	rules
il	**sacco a pelo**	sleeping bag
lo	**zaino**	rucksack

USEFUL PHRASES

andare in campeggio to go camping
accamparsi to camp
ben attrezzato(a) well equipped

ESSENTIAL WORDS *(feminine)*

l'	**acqua (non) potabile**	(non-)drinking water
la	**bombola del gas**	gas cylinder
la	**brandina**	camp bed
la	**campeggiatrice**	camper
la	**cassa**	box
la	**doccia** *(pl* **-ce***)*	shower
la	**forchetta**	fork
la	**lattina**	can, tin
la	**lavatrice**	washing machine
la	**notte**	night
la	**piazzola**	pitch, site
la	**pila**	torch, flashlight; battery
la	**piscina**	swimming pool
la	**roulotte** *(pl inv)*	caravan
la	**scatola**	box, tin
la	**(sedia a) sdraio**	deckchair
la	**sedia pieghevole**	folding chair
la	**stanza**	room
la	**tenda (da campeggio)**	tent
le	**toilette**	toilets

IMPORTANT WORDS *(feminine)*

la	**lavanderia**	launderette
l'	**ombra**	shade; shadow
la	**presa di corrente**	socket
la	**sala giochi**	games room

USEFUL PHRASES

montare una tenda to pitch a tent
fare salsicce alla griglia to grill sausages

careers

ESSENTIAL WORDS *(masculine)*

un	**agente di polizia**	policeman
un	**assistente di volo**	flight attendant
il	**capo**	boss
il	**carabiniere**	policeman
il	**cassiere**	check-out assistant
il	**commercio**	trade
il	**commesso**	sales assistant, shop assistant
il	**consulente professionale**	careers adviser
il	**datore di lavoro**	employer
il	**dipendente**	employee
il	**disegnatore di pagine web**	web designer
il	**dottore**	doctor
un	**elettricista**	electrician
il	**farmacista**	chemist
un	**impiegato**	clerk
un	**infermiere**	nurse
un	**ingegnere**	engineer
un	**insegnante**	teacher
il	**lavoro**	job; work
il	**macchinista**	train driver
il	**meccanico**	mechanic
il	**medico**	doctor
il	**poliziotto**	policeman
il	**pompiere**	fireman
il	**postino**	postman
il	**professore**	teacher
il	**programmatore**	computer programmer
il	**redattore**	editor
il	**soldato**	soldier
lo	**steward** *(pl inv)*	steward
un	**ufficio**	office
il	**vigile**	traffic warden

USEFUL PHRASES

interessante/poco interessante interesting/not very interesting
fa il postino he is a postman; **fa il medico** he/she is a doctor
lavorare to work; **diventare** to become

ESSENTIAL WORDS *(feminine)*

un' **ambizione**	ambition
un' **assistente di volo**	flight attendant
la **banca**	bank
la **cassiera**	check-out assistant
la **commessa**	sales assistant, shop assistant
la **consulente professionale**	careers adviser
la **dipendente**	employee
la **dottoressa**	doctor
la **fabbrica** *(pl* **-che***)*	factory
la **hostess** *(pl inv)*	stewardess
un' **impiegata**	clerk
un' **infermiera**	nurse
un' **insegnante**	teacher
la **paga**	wages
la **pensione**	retirement
la **postina**	postwoman
la **professione**	profession
la **professoressa**	teacher
la **programmatrice**	computer programmer
la **receptionist** *(pl inv)*	receptionist
la **redattrice**	editor
la **segretaria**	secretary
la **star** *(m+f pl inv)*	film star
la **vita**	life
la **vita lavorativa**	working life

USEFUL PHRASES

lavorare per guadagnarsi da vivere to work for one's living
che lavoro fa? what do you do (for a living)?
cosa vuoi fare da grande? what do you want to do when you grow up?
fare domanda di lavoro to apply for a job

careers

IMPORTANT WORDS *(masculine)*

gli	**affari**	business
l'	**apprendistato**	apprenticeship
un	**aumento**	rise
un	**autore**	author
il	**barbiere**	barber
il	**bidello**	caretaker, janitor *(at school)*
il	**collega** *(pl* **-ghi**)	colleague
il	**commerciante**	shopkeeper
il	**contratto**	contract
il	**cuoco** *(pl* **-chi**)	cook
il	**custode**	caretaker *(of building)*
il	**dirigente**	manager
il	**disoccupato**	unemployed person
il	**futuro**	future
un	**idraulico**	plumber
un	**imbianchino**	decorator
un	**impiego** *(pl* **-ghi**)	job; situation
un	**interinale**	temp
il	**lavoratore**	worker
il	**manager** *(pl inv)*	manager
il	**mercato del lavoro**	job market
un	**operaio**	worker
un	**ottico**	optician
il	**parrucchiere**	hairdresser
il	**pilota**	pilot
il	**pittore**	painter
il	**pompiere**	fireman
il	**posto di lavoro**	job
il	**presidente**	president; chairperson
lo	**sciopero**	strike
il	**sindacato**	trade union
un	**uomo d'affari**	businessman

USEFUL PHRASES

essere disoccupato(a) to be unemployed
licenziare qn per eccesso di personale to make sb redundant
un contratto a tempo indeterminato a permanent contract
un contratto a tempo determinato temporary contract

IMPORTANT WORDS *(feminine)*

un'	**agenzia di collocamento**	job centre
un'	**agenzia di lavoro temporaneo**	temping agency
la	**biblioteca** *(pl* **-che***)*	library
la	**bidella**	caretaker, janitor *(at school)*
la	**carriera**	career
la	**collega** *(pl* **-ghi***)*	colleague
la	**cuoca** *(pl* **-che***)*	cook
la	**custode**	caretaker *(of building)*
la	**dirigente**	manager
la	**disoccupazione**	unemployment
la	**domanda**	application
la	**donna d'affari**	businesswoman
la	**donna delle pulizie**	cleaner
un'	**interinale**	temp
la	**lettera d'accompagnamento**	covering letter
la	**manager** *(pl inv)*	manager
un'	**operaia**	worker
la	**parrucchiera**	hairdresser
la	**pittrice**	painter
la	**politica**	politics
la	**presidente**	president; chairperson

USEFUL PHRASES

"domande di impiego" "situations wanted"
"offerte di impiego" "situations vacant"
appartenere ad un sindacato to be in a union
guadagnare 1000 euro al mese to earn 1000 euros per month
un aumento (di paga) a pay rise
scioperare *or* **fare sciopero** to go on strike
essere in sciopero to be on strike
lavorare a tempo pieno/lavorare part-time to work full-time/to work part-time
fare lo straordinario to work overtime
riduzione delle ore lavorative reduction in working hours

USEFUL WORDS *(masculine)*

un	**agricoltore**	farmer *(crops)*
un	**allevatore**	farmer *(animals)*
un	**architetto**	architect
un	**artista**	artist
un	**avvocato**	lawyer; solicitor
il	**chirurgo** *(pl* **-ghi***)*	surgeon
il	**colloquio (di lavoro)**	(job) interview
il	**contabile**	accountant
il	**corso di formazione**	training course
il	**cosmonauta**	cosmonaut
il	**deputato**	MP
il	**direttore amministrativo**	company secretary
un	**elettrauto**	car electrician
il	**falegname**	joiner, carpenter
il	**fotografo**	photographer
il	**funzionario**	civil servant
il	**giornalista**	journalist
il	**giudice**	judge
un	**ingegnere**	engineer
un	**interprete**	interpreter
il	**marinaio**	sailor
il	**minatore**	miner
il	**modello**	model
il	**muratore**	bricklayer; mason
il	**notaio**	notary
il	**personale**	staff
il	**politico**	politician
il	**prete**	priest
il	**rappresentante**	sales rep
un	**ricercatore**	researcher
lo	**scrittore**	writer
lo	**stilista**	fashion designer
il	**sussidio di disoccupazione**	unemployment benefit
il	**tassista**	taxi driver
il	**tirocinio**	apprenticeship; training
il	**traduttore**	translator
il	**veterinario**	vet
il	**viticoltore**	wine grower

USEFUL WORDS *(feminine)*

un'	**agente di polizia**	policewoman
un'	**amministrazione**	administration
un'	**annunciatrice**	announcer
un'	**artista**	artist
la	**casalinga** *(pl* **-ghe***)*	housewife, home maker
la	**cassa integrazione**	redundancy payment
la	**contabile**	accountant
la	**deputata**	MP
la	**direttrice amministrativa**	company secretary
la	**ditta**	business
la	**formazione**	training
la	**giornalista**	journalist
un'	**impresa**	company; business
un'	**interprete**	interpreter
la	**modella**	model
la	**monaca** *(pl* **-che***)*	nun
la	**poliziotta**	policewoman
la	**rappresentante**	rep; sales rep
la	**sarta**	dressmaker
la	**società** *(pl inv)*	company
la	**suora**	nun
la	**traduttrice**	translator
la	**vigile**	traffic warden

USEFUL PHRASES

un lavoro stagionale seasonal work
un lavoro temporaneo/fisso a temporary/permanent job
un lavoro part-time a part-time job
essere assunto(a) to be taken on; **essere licenziato(a)** to be dismissed
licenziare qn to give sb the sack
cercare lavoro to look for work
fare un corso di formazione professionale to go on a training course
timbrare il cartellino to clock in/out
lavorare con un orario flessibile to work flexi-time

ESSENTIAL WORDS *(masculine)*

l'	**acceleratore**	accelerator
un	**agente di polizia**	policeman
un	**autista**	driver; chauffeur
un	**autovelox** *(pl inv)*	speed camera
il	**box** *(pl inv)*	garage *(for parking car)*
il	**cambio**	gear, gearbox
il	**chilometro**	kilometre
il	**ciclista**	cyclist
il	**distributore di benzina**	filling station; petrol pump
i	**fari**	headlights
il	**freno**	brake
il	**garage** *(pl inv)*	garage *(for parking car)*
il	**gasolio**	diesel
il	**guidatore**	driver
un	**incrocio**	crossroads
un	**ingorgo** *(pl* **-ghi***)*	traffic jam
il	**libretto di circolazione**	(car) registration document
il	**litro**	litre
il	**meccanico**	mechanic
il	**motore**	engine
il	**numero**	number
l'	**olio**	oil
il	**parcheggio**	car park
il	**pedaggio**	toll
il	**pedone**	pedestrian
lo	**pneumatico**	tyre
il	**semaforo**	traffic lights
lo	**svincolo autostradale**	motorway exit, junction
il	**viaggio**	journey

USEFUL PHRASES

frenare bruscamente to brake suddenly
100 chilometri all'ora 100 kilometres an hour
ha la patente? do you have a driving licence?
andiamo a fare un giro (in macchina) we're going for a drive (in the car)

ESSENTIAL WORDS *(feminine)*

l'	**acqua**	water
un'	**assicurazione**	insurance
un'	**autista**	driver; chauffeur
un'	**autorimessa**	garage *(for repairs)*
un'	**autostrada**	motorway
la	**benzina**	petrol
la	**benzina senza piombo**	unleaded petrol
la	**carta stradale**	street map
la	**deviazione**	diversion
la	**direzione**	direction
la	**distanza**	distance
la	**gomma**	tyre
la	**guidatrice**	driver
le	**indicazioni**	directions
la	**macchina**	car
la	**patente**	driving licence
la	**polizia**	police
la	**polizza di assicurazione**	insurance policy
la	**roulotte** *(pl inv)*	caravan
la	**stazione di servizio**	service station
la	**strada**	road
la	**strada principale**	main road
la	**strada statale**	main road; A road
la	**targa** *(pl* **-ghe***)*	number plate
un'	**uscita (autostradale)**	motorway exit, junction

USEFUL PHRASES

il pieno, per favore fill it up please
prendere la strada per Lecco to take the road to Lecco
è un viaggio di tre ore it's a 3-hour journey
buon viaggio! have a good journey!
andiamo! let's go!
lungo la strada abbiamo visto ... on the way we saw ...
sorpassare una macchina to overtake a car

cars

IMPORTANT WORDS *(masculine)*

un	**autolavaggio**	car wash
un	**automobilista**	motorist
l'	**autostop**	hitch-hiking
un	**autostoppista**	hitch-hiker
il	**bagagliaio**	boot
il	**benzinaio**	petrol pump attendant
il	**camionista**	lorry driver
il	**carro attrezzi**	breakdown van
il	**cartello stradale**	road sign
il	**clacson** *(pl inv)*	horn
il	**codice della strada**	highway code
il	**confine**	border
il	**cruscotto**	dashboard
il	**danno**	damage
i	**documenti (della macchina)**	official papers
il	**faro**	headlight
il	**guasto**	breakdown
un	**incidente (stradale)**	(road) accident
il	**motociclista**	motorcyclist
il	**parcheggio**	parking
il	**pezzo di ricambio**	spare part
lo	**scontro**	collision
il	**traffico**	traffic

USEFUL PHRASES

accendere il motore to switch on the engine
il motore parte the engine starts up
il motore non parte the engine won't start
accelerare to accelerate; **proseguire** to continue
ridurre la velocità to slow down
fermarsi to stop; **parcheggiare (la macchina)** to park (the car)
spegnere il motore to switch off the engine
fermarsi con il semaforo rosso to stop at the red light

IMPORTANT WORDS *(feminine)*

un'	**automobile**	car
un'	**automobilista**	motorist
un'	**autoscuola**	driving school
un'	**autostoppista**	hitch-hiker
la	**batteria**	battery
la	**carrozzeria**	body work
la	**cintura di sicurezza**	seat belt
la	**collisione**	collision
la	**foratura**	puncture
la	**frizione**	clutch
la	**marca** *(pl* **-che**)	make *(of car)*
la	**marcia** *(pl* **-ce**)	gear
la	**motociclista**	motorcyclist
la	**pompa di benzina**	petrol pump
la	**portiera**	(car) door
la	**prova del palloncino**	Breathalyser® test
la	**revisione**	MOT test
la	**rotatoria**	roundabout
la	**rotonda**	roundabout
la	**ruota di scorta**	spare tyre
la	**scuola guida**	driving school
la	**strada a senso unico**	one-way street
la	**velocità**	speed
la	**zona a traffico limitato**	controlled traffic zone
la	**zona pedonale**	pedestrian zone

USEFUL PHRASES

c'è stato un incidente there's been an accident
nell'incidente sono rimaste ferite sei persone six people were injured in the accident
favorisce i documenti, per cortesia? may I see your papers please?
forare to have a puncture; **riparare** to fix
avere un'avaria to break down
sono rimasto senza benzina I've run out of petrol

USEFUL WORDS *(masculine)*

il	**carabiniere**	policeman
il	**carburatore**	carburettor
il	**catalizzatore**	catalytic converter
il	**centro abitato**	built-up area
il	**certificato di assicurazione**	insurance certificate
il	**cofano**	bonnet
il	**consumo di benzina**	petrol consumption
il	**contachilometri** *(pl inv)*	speedometer
un	**istruttore di guida**	driving instructor
il	**lavaggio auto**	car-wash
il	**limite di velocità**	speed limit
il	**navigatore satellitare**	satellite navigation system (satnav)
il	**parabrezza** *(pl inv)*	windscreen
il	**paraurti** *(pl inv)*	bumper
il	**parchimetro**	parking meter
il	**pedale**	pedal
il	**portapacchi** *(pl inv)*	roof rack
il	**principiante**	learner driver
il	**pulsante di avvio**	starter
il	**rimorchio**	trailer
il	**servosterzo**	power steering
il	**(sistema di navigazione) GPS**	satellite navigation system
lo	**spartitraffico** *(pl inv)*	central reservation
lo	**specchietto retrovisore**	rear-view mirror
il	**tergicristalli** *(pl inv)*	windscreen wiper
il	**vigile**	traffic warden
il	**volante**	steering wheel

USEFUL PHRASES

a rimorchio on tow
nell'ora di punta at rush hour
ha ricevuto una multa di 100 euro he got a 100-euro fine
è assicurato? are you insured?
non dimentichi di allacciare le cinture di sicurezza don't forget to put on your seat belts
al confine at the border
fare l'autostop to hitch-hike

USEFUL WORDS *(feminine)*

un'	**area di servizio**	service station
la	**rampa d'accesso**	slip road
la	**circonvallazione**	ring road
la	**corsia**	lane
la	**corsia d'emergenza**	hard shoulder
la	**curva**	bend
la	**deviazione**	detour
la	**freccia** *(pl* **-ce***)*	indicator
la	**frenata improvvisa**	emergency stop
un'	**infrazione stradale**	traffic offence
la	**lezione di guida**	driving lesson
la	**multa**	fine
la	**piazzola di sosta**	lay-by
la	**pressione**	pressure
la	**stazione di servizio**	service station
la	**via**	street
la	**vigile**	traffic warden
la	**vittima**	casualty

USEFUL PHRASES

la ruota anteriore/posteriore the front/back wheel
dobbiamo fare una deviazione we have to make a detour
una multa per eccesso di velocità a fine for speeding
accosti per favore pull in please
"dare la precedenza" "give way to the right"
"tenere la destra" "keep to the right"
"vietato l'accesso" "no entry"
"divieto di sosta" "no parking"
"lavori in corso" "roadworks"

ESSENTIAL WORDS *(masculine)*

l'	**abito**	suit; dress
il	**bottone**	button
il	**calzino**	sock
i	**calzoni**	trousers
il	**cappello**	hat
il	**cappotto**	coat
i	**collant**	tights
il	**costume da bagno**	swimming trunks; swimsuit
il	**fazzoletto**	handkerchief
un	**impermeabile**	raincoat
i	**jeans**	jeans
il	**maglione**	jumper
il	**numero (di scarpe)**	(shoe) size
un	**ombrello**	umbrella
i	**pantaloncini**	shorts
i	**pantaloni**	trousers
il	**pigiama**	pyjamas
il	**reggiseno**	bra
gli	**slip** *(pl inv)*	knickers; underpants
il	**soprabito**	overcoat
i	**vestiti**	clothes
il	**vestito**	suit; dress; costume

IMPORTANT WORDS *(masculine)*

un	**accappatoio**	bathrobe
il	**cappuccio**	hood
il	**giaccone**	heavy jacket
il	**golf** *(pl inv)*	cardigan
il	**guanto**	glove
i	**pantaloni corti**	shorts
il	**sandalo**	sandal
lo	**scarpone**	boot
gli	**shorts**	shorts
gli	**stivali**	boots

ESSENTIAL WORDS *(feminine)*

la	**biancheria intima**	underwear
la	**borsa**	bag
la	**borsetta**	handbag
la	**camicia**	shirt
la	**camicia da notte**	nightdress
la	**cravatta**	tie
la	**felpa**	sweatshirt
la	**giacca** *(pl* **-che***)*	jacket
la	**giacca** *(pl* **-che***)* **a vento**	anorak
la	**gonna**	skirt
la	**maglietta**	T-shirt
la	**moda**	fashion
le	**mutande**	underpants; knickers
la	**scarpa**	shoe
la	**taglia**	size
la	**vita**	waist

IMPORTANT WORDS *(feminine)*

la	**blusa**	blouse
la	**canottiera**	vest
la	**ciabatta**	slipper
la	**cintura**	belt
la	**roba da vestire**	clothes
la	**tasca**	pocket
un'	**uniforme**	uniform
la	**vestaglia**	dressing gown

USEFUL PHRASES

di mattina mi vesto in the morning I get dressed
di sera mi spoglio in the evening I get undressed
quando torno a casa da scuola mi cambio when I get home from school I get changed
indossare *or* **avere addosso** to wear
mettersi to put on
è molto elegante that's very smart

clothes

USEFUL WORDS *(masculine)*

gli **accessori**	accessories
il **bastone (da passeggio)**	walking stick
i **bermuda**	Bermuda shorts
il **berretto**	cap; beret
il **bucato**	washing
il **camice**	overalls
il **colletto**	collar
il **fascinator** *(pl inv)*	fascinator
il **fiocco** *(pl* **-chi***)*	bow
il **foulard** *(pl inv)*	scarf
il **gilè** *(pl inv)*	waistcoat
il **grembiule**	apron
gli **infradito**	flip flops
i **lacci**	(shoe)laces
il **nastro**	ribbon
un **occhiello**	buttonhole
il **papillon** *(pl inv)*	bow tie
lo **spogliatoio**	changing room
il **vestito da sera**	evening dress
il **vestito da sposa**	wedding dress

USEFUL PHRASES

ti sta bene that suits you
che taglia porti (*or* **porta)?** what size do you take?
che numero di scarpe porti (*or* **porta)?** what shoe size do you take?
ho il 38 di piede I take size 38 in shoes

USEFUL WORDS *(feminine)*

l'	**alta moda**	haute couture
la	**(borsa a) tracolla**	shoulder bag
le	**bretelle**	braces
le	**calze**	stockings; socks
la	**canotta**	tank top
la	**chiusura lampo** *(pl* **-e ~***)*	zip
la	**felpa**	sweatshirt
la	**gonna pantalone**	culottes
la	**maglia con il cappuccio**	hooded top
la	**maglietta senza maniche**	tank top
la	**manica** *(pl* **-che***)*	sleeve
la	**polo** *(pl inv)*	polo shirt
la	**pulitura a secco**	dry-cleaning
la	**salopette** *(pl inv)*	dungarees
le	**scarpe basse**	flat shoes
le	**scarpe con i tacchi**	high heels
le	**scarpe da ginnastica**	trainers
la	**sfilata di moda**	fashion show
la	**sottogonna**	underskirt
la	**tuta da ginnastica**	tracksuit
la	**zip** *(pl inv)*	zip

USEFUL PHRASES

lungo(a) long; **corto(a)** short
un vestito con le maniche corte/lunghe a short-sleeved/long-sleeved dress
stretto(a) tight
largo(a) loose
una gonna attillata a tight skirt
a strisce striped; **a quadretti** checked; **a pallini** spotted
vestiti sportivi casual clothes
in pigiama in pyjamas
alla moda fashionable; **moderno(a)** trendy
fuori moda old-fashioned

arancione	orange
azzurro(a)	light blue
beige *(pl inv)*	beige
bianco(a)	white
blu *(pl inv)*	blue
blu marina *(pl inv)*	navy blue
blu scuro *(pl inv)*	dark blue
bordeaux *(pl inv)*	maroon
celeste	sky blue
d'argento *(pl inv)*	silver
dorato(a)	golden
d'oro *(pl inv)*	gold
giallo(a)	yellow
grigio(a)	grey
malva *(pl inv)*	mauve
marrone	brown
naturale	natural
nero(a)	black
rosa *(pl inv)*	pink
rosso(a)	red
rosso fuoco *(pl inv)*	bright red
turchese	turquoise
verde	green
viola *(pl inv)*	purple
violetto(a)	violet

USEFUL PHRASES

il colore colour
di che colore hai (*or* ha) gli occhi/i capelli? what colour are your eyes/is your hair?
il blu ti sta bene blue suits you
quello blu ti sta bene the blue one suits you
dipingere qc di blu to paint sth blue
le scarpe blu blue shoes
le scarpe azzurre light blue shoes
ha gli occhi verdi she/he has green eyes
cambiare colore to change colour
la Casa Bianca the White House
un (uomo) bianco a white man
una (donna) bianca a white woman
un (uomo) nero a black man
una (donna) nera a black woman
bianco come la neve as white as snow
Biancaneve Snow White
Cappuccetto Rosso Little Red Riding Hood
diventare rosso(a) to turn red, to blush
rosso(a) come un peperone as red as a beetrot
chiaro(a)/scuro(a) light/dark
nero(a) come il carbone as brown as a berry
un occhio nero a black eye
un (romanzo) giallo a crime novel
un romanzo rosa a romantic novel
Pagine Gialle Yellow pages
una notte in bianco a sleepless night
riso/pasta in bianco plain rice/pasta
la benzina verde unleaded petrol
numero verde freephone
essere al verde to be broke
essere di umore nero to be in a very bad mood

computing and IT

ESSENTIAL WORDS *(masculine)*

il	**computer** *(pl inv)*	computer
il	**mouse** *(pl inv)*	mouse
il	**programma**	program

USEFUL WORDS *(masculine)*

l'	**ADSL**	broadband
il	**backup** *(pl inv)*	back-up
il	**blog** *(pl inv)*	blog
il	**browser** *(pl inv)*	browser
il	**CD-ROM** *(pl inv)*	CD-ROM
il	**cloud**	cloud
il	**cloud computing**	cloud computing
il	**correttore ortografico**	spellchecker
il	**cursore**	cursor
i	**dati**	data
il	**disco rigido**	hard disk
il	**documento**	document
il	**dongle** *(pl inv)*	dongle
il	**file** *(pl inv)*	file
il	**foglio di calcolo**	spreadsheet
un	**indirizzo di posta elettronica**	email address
	Internet	internet
il	**libro elettronico**	e-book
il	**menu** *(pl inv)*	menu
il	**messaggio di posta elettronica**	email message
il	**microblog** *(pl inv)*	microblog
il	**monitor** *(pl inv)*	monitor
il	**pirata informatico**	hacker
il	**portatile**	laptop
il	**router wifi** *(pl inv)*	wifi router
lo	**schermo**	screen
il	**sito web**	website
il	**social media**	social media
il	**social network** *(pl inv)*	social networking site
il	**software** *(pl inv)*	software
il	**virus** *(pl inv)*	virus
il	**Web**	Web

ESSENTIAL WORDS *(feminine)*

l'	**informatica**	computer science
la	**stampante**	printer

USEFUL WORDS *(feminine)*

un'	**applicazione**	program, app
la	**banda larga**	broadband
la	**cartuccia d'inchiostro**	ink cartridge
la	**chiavetta USB**	USB key
la	**copia di sicurezza**	back-up
la	**finestra**	window
la	**funzione**	function
la	**home page** *(pl inv)*	home page
un'	**icona**	icon
un'	**interfaccia** *(pl* **-ce***)*	interface
la	**mail** *(pl inv)*	email (message)
la	**memoria**	memory
la	**(memoria) RAM**	RAM, random-access memory
la	**(memoria) ROM**	ROM, read-only memory
la	**navigatrice internet**	internet user
la	**password** *(pl inv)*	password
la	**posta elettronica**	email
la	**rete**	network
la	**scheda di memoria**	memory stick
la	**stampa**	print-out
la	**tastiera**	keyboard
un'	**unità disco** *(pl inv)*	disk drive
la	**webcam** *(pl inv)*	webcam
il	**wireless**	wireless

USEFUL PHRASES

copiare to copy; **cancellare** to delete
formattare to format
scaricare/caricare un file to download/upload a file
salvare to save; **stampare** to print; **digitare** to key
visualizzare to view
navigare in Internet to surf the internet

ESSENTIAL WORDS *(masculine)*

il **Belgio**	Belgium
il **Canada**	Canada
il **Galles**	Wales
il **paese**	country; village
i **Paesi Bassi**	Netherlands
il **Regno Unito**	United Kingdom
gli **Stati Uniti**	United States
il **Sudamerica**	South America
gli **USA**	USA

USEFUL WORDS *(masculine)*

il **Brasile**	Brazil
El **Salvador**	El Salvador
il **Giappone**	Japan
il **Marocco**	Morocco
il **Messico**	Mexico
il **Pakistan**	Pakistan
il **Perù**	Peru
il **Terzo Mondo**	Third World

USEFUL PHRASES

il mio paese d'origine my native country
la capitale italiana the capital of Italy
di che paese sei? what country do you come from?
sono italiano/canadese I am Italian/Canadian
sono nato in Scozia I was born in Scotland
vado nei Paesi Bassi I'm going to the Netherlands
sono appena tornato dagli Stati Uniti I've just come back from the United States
sei mai stato in Italia? have you ever been to Italy?
i paesi in via di sviluppo the developing countries
i paesi di lingua spagnola Spanish-speaking countries

ESSENTIAL WORDS *(feminine)*

l' **America**	America
l' **Europa**	Europe
la **Francia**	France
la **Germania**	Germany
la **Gran Bretagna**	Great Britain
l' **Inghilterra**	England
l' **Irlanda (del Nord)**	(Northern) Ireland
l' **Italia**	Italy
l' **Olanda**	Holland
la **Scozia**	Scotland
la **Spagna**	Spain
la **Svizzera**	Switzerland

USEFUL WORDS *(feminine)*

l' **Africa**	Africa
l' **Algeria**	Algeria
l' **America del sud**	South America
l' **Asia**	Asia
l' **Australia**	Australia
l' **Austria**	Austria
la **Cina**	China
la **Croazia**	Croatia
la **Finlandia**	Finland
la **Grecia**	Greece
l' **India**	India
la **Norvegia**	Norway
la **Nuova Zelanda**	New Zealand
la **Russia**	Russia
la **Slovenia**	Slovenia
la **Tunisia**	Tunisia
l' **Ungheria**	Hungary
l' **Unione europea, la UE**	the European Union, the EU

countries and nationalities

ESSENTIAL WORDS *(masculine)*

un	**americano**	an American
un	**belga**	a Belgian
un	**britannico**	a Briton
un	**canadese**	a Canadian
un	**europeo**	a European
un	**francese**	a Frenchman
un	**gallese**	a Welshman
un	**inglese**	an Englishman
un	**irlandese**	an Irishman
un	**italiano**	an Italian
un	**olandese**	a Dutchman
un	**pachistano**	a Pakistani
uno	**scozzese**	a Scot
uno	**spagnolo**	a Spaniard
uno	**svizzero**	a Swiss (man *or* boy)
un	**tedesco** *(pl* **-chi***)*	a German
un	**ungherese**	a Hungarian

USEFUL PHRASES

è irlandese he/she is Irish
la campagna irlandese the Irish countryside
una città irlandese an Irish town

ESSENTIAL WORDS *(feminine)*

un' **americana**	an American
una **belga**	a Belgian
una **britannica** *(pl* **-che***)*	a Briton, a British woman *or* girl
una **canadese**	a Canadian
un' **europea**	a European
una **francese**	a Frenchwoman, a French girl
una **gallese**	a Welshwoman, a Welsh girl
un' **inglese**	an Englishwoman, an English girl
un' **irlandese**	an Irishwoman, an Irish girl
un' **italiana**	an Italian
un' **olandese**	a Dutchwoman, a Dutch girl
una **pachistana**	a Pakistani
una **scozzese**	a Scot
una **spagnola**	a Spaniard
una **svizzera**	a Swiss woman *or* girl
una **tedesca** *(pl* **-che***)*	a German
un' **ungherese**	a Hungarian

USEFUL PHRASES

parlo inglese I speak English
sono scozzese I am Scottish
uno(a) straniero(a) a foreigner
all'estero abroad
la nazionalità nationality

USEFUL WORDS *(masculine)*

un **africano**	an African
un **albanese**	an Albanian
un **arabo**	an Arab
un **argentino**	an Argentinian
un **asiatico** *(pl* **-chi***)*	an Asian
un **australiano**	an Australian
un **caraibico** *(pl* **-chi***)*	a West Indian
un **ceco** *(pl* **-chi***)*	a Czech
un **cinese**	a Chinese
un **giapponese**	a Japanese
un **indiano**	an Indian
un **neozelandese**	a New Zealander
un **portoghese**	a Portuguese
un **polacco** *(pl* **-chi***)*	a Pole
un **russo**	a Russian
un **slovacco** *(pl* **-chi***)*	a Slovakian
un **turco** *(pl* **-chi***)*	a Turk
un **ucraino**	a Ukranian

USEFUL WORDS *(feminine)*

un' **africana**	an African
un' **albanese**	an Albanian
un' **araba**	an Arab
un' **argentina**	an Argentinian
un' **asiatica** *(pl* **-che***)*	an Asian
un' **australiana**	an Australian
una **caraibica** *(pl* **-che***)*	a West Indian
una **ceca** *(pl* **-che***)*	a Czech
una **cinese**	a Chinese
una **giapponese**	a Japanese
un' **indiana**	an Indian
una **neozelandese**	a New Zealander
una **polacca** *(pl* **-che***)*	a Pole
una **portoghese**	a Portuguese
una **russa**	a Russian
una **slovacca** *(pl* **-che***)*	a Slovakian
una **turca** *(pl* **-che***)*	a Turk
un' **ucraina**	a Ukranian

ESSENTIAL WORDS *(masculine)*

un	**albero**	tree
un	**allevatore**	farmer *(raising animals)*
il	**bastone (da passeggio)**	walking stick
il	**bosco** *(pl* **-chi***)*	wood; forest
il	**cacciatore**	hunter
il	**campo**	field
il	**cancello**	gate
il	**castello**	castle
il	**contadino**	farmer *(growing crops)*
il	**fiume**	river
il	**furgone**	van
il	**mercato**	market
un	**ostello della gioventù**	youth hostel
il	**paesaggio**	scenery
il	**paese**	village
il	**picnic** *(pl inv)*	picnic
il	**ponte**	bridge
il	**prato**	meadow
il	**rifugio**	mountain hostel
il	**rumore**	noise
il	**ruscello**	stream
il	**sasso**	stone, pebble
il	**sentiero**	path; track
lo	**steccato**	fence
il	**suolo**	ground
il	**terreno**	land; ground
il	**turista**	tourist

USEFUL PHRASES

all'aria aperta in the open air
so come arrivare al paese I know the way to the village
andare in bicicletta to go cycling
gli abitanti del posto the locals
siamo andati a fare un picnic we went for a picnic

ESSENTIAL WORDS *(feminine)*

un'	**allevatrice**	farmer *(raising animals)*
l'	**aria**	air
la	**cacciatrice**	hunter
la	**campagna**	country; countryside
la	**contadina**	farmer *(growing crops)*
un'	**escursione**	hike
la	**fattoria**	farm, farmhouse
la	**montagna**	mountain
la	**passeggiata**	walk
la	**pietra**	stone
la	**regione**	district
la	**roccia** *(pl* **-ce***)*	rock
la	**strada**	way; road
la	**terra**	land; earth; soil; ground
la	**torre**	tower
la	**turista**	tourist
la	**valle**	valley

USEFUL PHRASES

in campagna in the country
andare in campagna to go into the country
vivere in campagna/in città to live in the country/in town
coltivare la terra to cultivate the land

IMPORTANT WORDS *(masculine)*

il	**fienile**	barn
il	**fiore**	flower
il	**lago** *(pl* **-ghi***)*	lake
il	**podere**	farm; holding
gli	**stivali di gomma**	(wellington) boots
il	**vigneto**	vineyard

USEFUL WORDS *(masculine)*

un	**agriturismo**	farm where you can have holiday
un	**arbusto**	bush
il	**bastone**	stick
il	**binocolo**	binoculars
il	**borgo**	hamlet
il	**cartello segnaletico**	signpost
il	**cespuglio**	bush
il	**ciottolo**	pebble
il	**fango**	mud
il	**fieno**	hay
il	**fossato**	ditch
il	**furgone**	van
il	**grano**	grain; wheat
il	**mulino (a vento)**	(wind)mill
il	**palo della luce**	telegraph pole
il	**pozzo**	well
il	**prato**	meadow
il	**raccolto**	crop; harvest
lo	**stagno**	pond

USEFUL PHRASES

agricolo(a) agricultural
tranquillo(a) peaceful
in cima alla collina at the top of the hill
cadere in trappola to fall into a trap

IMPORTANT WORDS *(feminine)*

l'	**agricoltura**	agriculture
la	**cima**	top *(of hill)*
la	**collina**	hill
la	**foglia**	leaf
la	**gente di campagna**	country people
la	**pace**	peace, tranquillity
la	**polvere**	dust
la	**proprietà**	property; estate
la	**stalla**	stable
la	**tranquillità**	tranquillity, peace
la	**trattoria**	restaurant *(in country)*
la	**vigna**	vineyard
la	**vista**	view

USEFUL WORDS *(feminine)*

la	**brughiera**	moor
la	**caccia**	hunting
la	**cascata**	waterfall
la	**cava**	quarry
l'	**erica** *(pl* **-che**)	heather
la	**fonte**	spring; source
la	**grotta**	cave
la	**palude**	marsh
la	**pianura**	plain
la	**pozzanghera**	puddle
la	**riva**	bank *(of river)*
le	**rovine**	ruins
la	**siepe**	hedge
la	**trappola**	trap
la	**vendemmia**	grape harvest

USEFUL PHRASES

perdersi to lose one's way; to get lost
raccogliere frutta, grano to harvest fruit, grain
vendemmiare, fare la vendemmia to harvest the grapes

describing people

ESSENTIAL WORDS *(masculine)*

un **aspetto**	appearance
i **baffi**	moustache
i **capelli**	hair
il **colore**	colour
gli **occhi**	eyes

USEFUL PHRASES

allegro(a) cheerful
alto(a) tall
antipatico(a) unpleasant
basso(a) short
bello handsome; **bella** beautiful *(person)*
beneducato(a) well-behaved
brutto(a) ugly
buono(a) kind
calvo(a) bald
carino(a) pretty; cute
cattivo(a) naughty
con la barba bearded, with a beard
dinamico(a) dynamic
divertente amusing, entertaining; funny
educato(a) polite
felice happy
giovane young
grasso(a) fat
infelice unhappy
inquieto(a) agitated
intelligente intelligent
lungo(a) long
magro(a) thin
maleducato(a) rude
nervoso(a) nervous
orribile hideous

ESSENTIAL WORDS *(feminine)*

la	**barba**	beard
l'	**età**	age
l'	**identità**	identity
gli	**occhiali**	glasses
la	**persona**	person
la	**pettinatura**	hairstyle
la	**statura**	height
la	**taglia**	size

USEFUL PHRASES

ottimista/pessimista optimistic/pessimistic
piccolo(a) small, little
serio(a) serious
sfortunato(a) unfortunate
simpatico(a) nice
snello(a) slim
stupendo(a) great
stupido(a) stupid
teso(a) tense
timido(a) shy
tranquillo(a) calm
vecchio(a) old
ha un'aria triste he/she looks sad
stava piangendo he/she was crying
stava sorridendo he/she was smiling
aveva le lacrime agli occhi he/she had tears in his eyes
un uomo di statura media a man of average height
sono alto 1 metro e 70 *or* **uno e settanta** I am 1 metre 70 tall
di che colore hai (*or* **ha) gli occhi/i capelli?** what colour are your eyes/is your hair?
ho i capelli chiari I have fair hair
ho gli occhi azzurri/verdi I have blue/green eyes
capelli castano chiaro light brown hair; **capelli ricci** curly hair; **con i capelli rossi** red-haired
capelli neri/grigi black/grey hair
capelli scuri/castani dark/brown hair
capelli tinti dyed hair

IMPORTANT WORDS *(masculine)*

il **brufolo**	spot; pimple
il **carattere**	character; nature
lo **sguardo**	look
il **sorriso**	smile
l' **umore**	mood

USEFUL WORDS *(masculine)*

il **difetto**	fault
il **foruncolo**	spot, zit; boil
il **gesto**	gesture
il **gigante**	giant
il **neo**	mole, beauty spot
il **peso**	weight
il **ricciolo**	curl

USEFUL PHRASES

ha un buon carattere he/she is goodnatured
avere la carnagione chiara to have a pale complexion
portare gli occhiali to wear glasses
portare le lenti a contatto to wear contact lenses

IMPORTANT WORDS *(feminine)*

un'	**abitudine**	habit
la	**bellezza**	beauty
la	**bruttezza**	ugliness
la	**carnagione**	complexion
la	**curiosità**	curiosity
un'	**espressione**	expression
le	**lenti a contatto**	contact lenses
la	**qualità**	(good) quality
la	**vita**	waist
la	**voce**	voice

USEFUL WORDS *(feminine)*

la	**cicatrice**	scar
la	**dentiera**	false teeth
la	**fossetta**	dimple
la	**frangia**	fringe
le	**lentiggini**	freckles
la	**permanente**	perm
la	**rassomiglianza**	resemblance
le	**rughe**	wrinkles
la	**timidezza**	shyness

USEFUL PHRASES

sono sempre di buon umore I am always in a good mood
è di cattivo umore he/she is in a bad mood
si è arrabbiato he got angry
assomiglia a sua madre he/she looks like his/her mother
si mangia le unghie he/she bites his/her nails

ESSENTIAL WORDS *(masculine)*

l'	**alfabeto**	alphabet
un	**alunno**	pupil; schoolboy
un	**amico**	friend
un	**asilo**	nursery school
il	**compagno di classe**	classmate
i	**compiti (per casa)**	homework
il	**compito**	homework; task; test
il	**computer** *(pl inv)*	computer
il	**concerto**	concert
il	**disegno**	drawing
il	**dormitorio**	dormitory
un	**errore**	mistake
un	**esame**	exam
un	**esperimento**	experiment
il	**francese**	French
il	**giorno**	day
il	**gruppo**	group
l'	**inglese**	English
l'	**insegnamento**	education; teaching
l'	**intervallo**	break; playtime
un	**istituto (scolastico)**	school; institute
l'	**italiano**	Italian
il	**laboratorio**	laboratory
i	**lavori manuali**	handicrafts
il	**lavoro**	work
il	**libro**	book
il	**liceo**	secondary school *(16 to 18 year olds)*
il	**maestro**	primary school teacher
il	**nuoto**	swimming
un	**orario**	timetable
il	**premio**	prize
il	**preside**	headmaster
il	**professore**	teacher
il	**progresso**	progress
il	**quaderno**	exercise book
il	**refettorio**	dining hall

ESSENTIAL WORDS *(feminine)*

un'	**alunna**	pupil; schoolgirl
un'	**amica** *(pl* **-che***)*	friend
un'	**aula**	classroom
la	**biologia**	biology
la	**carta geografica** *(pl* **-e -che***)*	map
la	**chimica**	chemistry
la	**classe**	class; year; classroom
la	**compagna di classe**	school friend
la	**domanda**	question
l'	**educazione fisica**	PE
l'	**elettronica**	electronics
un'	**escursione**	trip; outing
la	**fisica**	physics
la	**frase**	sentence
la	**geografia**	geography
la	**ginnastica**	PE, gymnastics
la	**gomma (da cancellare)**	rubber
l'	**informatica**	computer studies
un'	**interrogazione**	oral test
la	**lavagna**	blackboard
la	**lavagna bianca**	whiteboard
la	**lettura**	reading
la	**lezione**	lesson
le	**lingue straniere**	(modern) languages
la	**maestra**	primary school teacher
la	**matematica**	mathematics, maths
la	**materia (scolastica)**	(school) subject
la	**matita**	pencil
la	**mensa**	canteen
la	**musica**	music
la	**palestra**	gym
la	**parola**	word
la	**penna**	pen
la	**piscina**	swimming pool
la	**presentazione**	presentation
la	**preside**	headmistress
la	**professoressa**	teacher
la	**ricreazione**	break; playtime

ESSENTIAL WORDS *(masculine continued)*

il **risultato**	result
lo **sbaglio**	mistake
lo **scambio**	exchange
lo **scolaro**	schoolboy
il **semestre**	semester
lo **spagnolo**	Spanish
lo **studente**	student
gli **studi**	studies
lo **studio**	study
il **tedesco**	German
il **tirocinio**	apprenticeship
il **voto**	mark

USEFUL PHRASES

lavorare to work
imparare to learn
studiare to study
da quanto tempo studi l'italiano? how long have you been learning Italian?
imparare qc a memoria to learn sth off by heart
ho compiti da fare tutti i giorni I have homework every day
la mia sorellina va alle elementari, io frequento la scuola secondaria my little sister goes to primary school – I go to secondary school
insegnare l'italiano to teach Italian
il professore/la professoressa di tedesco the German teacher
ho fatto progressi *or* **ho migliorato in matematica** I have made progress in maths
dare un esame to sit an exam
passare un esame to pass an exam
non passare un esame to fail an exam
essere interrogato(a) to have an oral test
prendere la sufficienza to get a pass mark

ESSENTIAL WORDS *(feminine continued)*

la	**risposta**	answer; reply
la	**sala professori**	staffroom
le	**scienze**	science
la	**scolara**	schoolgirl
la	**scuola**	school
la	**scuola secondaria**	secondary school
la	**scuola (secondaria) superiore**	secondary school *(14 to 19 year olds)*
la	**scuola elementare** *or* **primaria**	primary school
la	**scuola materna**	nursery school
la	**scuola media** *or* **secondaria inferiore**	secondary school *(11 to 14 year olds)*
la	**storia**	history; story
la	**studentessa**	student
un'	**università**	university
le	**vacanze**	holidays
le	**vacanze estive**	summer holidays

USEFUL PHRASES

facile easy; **difficile** difficult
interessante interesting
noioso(a) boring
leggere to read; **scrivere** to write
ascoltare to listen (to)
guardare to look at, watch
ripetere to repeat
rispondere to reply
parlare to speak
è la prima *or* **la migliore della classe** she is top of the class
è la peggiore della classe she is bottom of the class
entrare in classe to go into the classroom
fare un errore *or* **uno sbaglio** to make a mistake
correggere to correct
ho fatto un errore di grammatica I made a grammatical error
ho ricevuto un bel voto I got a good mark
rispondete alla domanda! answer the question!
alzate la mano! put your hand up!

IMPORTANT WORDS *(masculine)*

un	**astuccio portapenne**	pencil case
il	**certificato**	certificate
il	**corridoio**	corridor
il	**cortile (per la ricreazione)**	playground
il	**diploma**	diploma
il	**diploma di scuola secondaria**	higher school-leaving course/ certificate
un	**esame di ammissione**	entrance exam
l'	**esame di maturità**	school-leaving examination
un	**esame orale**	oral exam
un	**esame scritto**	written exam
il	**foglio di carta**	sheet of paper
il	**giorno libero**	day off
il	**libro elettronico**	e-book
il	**regolamento scolastico**	school rules
il	**righello**	ruler
un	**ufficio**	office
lo	**zaino**	rucksack; school bag

USEFUL PHRASES

il mio amico sta preparando l'esame di ammissione all'università my friend is sitting his university entrance exam

ripassare (la lezione) to revise

ripasserò la lezione ancora una volta domani I'll go over the lesson again tomorrow

IMPORTANT WORDS *(feminine)*

un' **assenza**	absence
la **carta**	paper
la **cartella**	folder; file; schoolbag
la **conferenza**	lecture
la **laurea**	university degree
la **pagella**	school report
la **regola**	rule
la **scuola privata**	private school
la **scuola statale**	state school
la **traduzione**	translation

USEFUL PHRASES

al secondo anno in year two
al primo anno della scuola media in year seven
al secondo anno della scuola media in year eight
al terzo anno della scuola media in year nine
al primo anno della scuola superiore in year ten
al secondo anno della scuola superiore in year eleven

presente present
assente absent
punire un alunno/un'alunna to punish a pupil
silenzio! be quiet!

USEFUL WORDS *(masculine)*

un	**alunno interno**	boarder
il	**banco** *(pl* **-chi***)*	(pupil's) desk
il	**bidello**	janitor
il	**bloc-notes** *(pl inv)*	jotter
il	**castigo** *(pl* **-ghi***)*	punishment
il	**collegio**	boarding school
il	**comportamento**	behaviour
il	**dizionario**	dictionary
un	**esaminatore**	examiner
un	**esercizio**	exercise
un	**evidenziatore**	highlighter
i	**gabinetti**	lavatories; cloakroom
il	**gesso**	chalk
il	**greco**	Greek
l'	**inchiostro**	ink
un	**insegnante di sostegno**	support teacher
un	**ispettore scolastico**	school inspector
il	**latino**	Latin
il	**libretto delle assenze**	absence sheet
il	**libro di testo**	textbook
il	**liquido correttore**	correction fluid
il	**pennarello**	felt-tip pen
il	**quadrimestre**	term (4 months)
il	**tema**	essay; class exam
il	**temperamatite** *(pl inv)*	pencil sharpener
il	**test** *(pl inv)*	test
il	**trimestre**	term (3 months)
il	**tutor** *(pl inv)*	form tutor
il	**vocabolario**	vocabulary; dictionary

USEFUL WORDS *(feminine)*

un'	**alunna interna**	boarder
l'	**algebra**	algebra
l'	**aritmetica**	arithmetic
la	**bidella**	janitor
la	**biro** *(pl inv)*	Biro®
la	**brutta copia**	rough copy
la	**calcolatrice**	calculator
la	**calligrafia**	handwriting
la	**cattedra**	teacher's desk
la	**facoltà** *(pl inv)*	faculty
la	**fila**	row *(of seats etc)*
la	**geometria**	geometry
la	**grammatica**	grammar
un'	**insegnante di sostegno**	support teacher
un'	**ispettrice scolastica** *(pl* **-i -che***)*	school inspector
la	**macchia**	blot
l'	**ortografia**	spelling
la	**poesia**	poetry; poem
la	**prova**	test
la	**religione**	religion; religious education, RE
le	**scienze naturali**	natural science
la	**scuola professionale**	technical college
la	**somma**	sum
la	**sufficienza**	pass mark; average mark

environment

ESSENTIAL WORDS *(masculine)*

gli **abitanti**	inhabitants
gli **alberi**	trees
l' **ambiente**	environment
gli **animali**	animals
il **bosco** *(pl* **-chi***)*	woods; forest
il **combustibile fossile**	fossil fuel
un **ecologista**	environmentalist
il **fiore**	flower
il **gas** *(pl inv)*	gas
i **gas di scarico**	exhaust fumes
il **gasolio**	diesel
l' **inquinamento**	pollution
il **mare**	sea
il **mondo**	world
i **pesci**	fish
il **tempo**	weather; time
i **Verdi**	the Greens
il **vetro**	glass

IMPORTANT WORDS *(masculine)*

un **agente inquinante**	pollutant
il **biocarburante**	biofuel
il **buco** *(pl* **-chi***)*	hole
il **calore**	heat
i **cambiamenti climatici**	climate change
il **clima**	climate
il **danno**	damage
il **detersivo**	detergent; washing powder
il **fiume**	river
il **futuro**	future
il **governo**	government
il **lago** *(pl* **-ghi***)*	lake
il **pannello solare**	solar panel
il **pianeta**	planet
il **vegetale**	vegetable

ESSENTIAL WORDS *(feminine)*

l' **acqua**	water
l' **aria**	air
un' **automobile**	car
la **benzina**	petrol
le **bottiglie**	bottles
la **campagna**	country
la **carta geografica** (*pl* **-e -che**)	map
la **costa**	coast
l' **ecologia**	ecology
l' **energia sostenibile**	renewable energy
la **fabbrica** (*pl* **-che**)	factory
la **frutta**	fruit
un' **isola**	island
la **macchina**	car
la **montagna**	mountain
la **pianta**	plant
la **pioggia** (*pl* **-ge**)	rain
la **questione**	question
la **regione**	region; area
la **specie** (*pl inv*)	species
la **spiaggia** (*pl* **-ge**)	beach
la **temperatura**	temperature
la **terra**	earth; soil; ground
la **verdura**	vegetables

IMPORTANT WORDS *(feminine)*

la **centrale eolica** (*pl* **-i -che**)	windfarm
la **centrale nucleare**	nuclear plant
la **foresta**	forest
la **giungla**	jungle
un' **imposta**	tax
la **impronta di carbonio**	carbon footprint
la **pala eolica**	wind turbine
la **tassa**	tax
la **turbina eolica**	wind turbine
la **zona**	zone

USEFUL WORDS *(masculine)*

l'	**alluminio**	aluminium
un	**avvenimento**	event
il	**buco dell'ozono**	ozone hole
il	**canale**	canal
i	**CFC (clorofluorocarburi)**	CFCs
i	**cibi biologici**	organic food
il	**combustibile**	fuel
il	**continente**	continent
il	**deserto**	desert
l'	**ecosistema**	ecosystem
il	**fertilizzante**	(artificial) fertilizer
un	**inceneritore**	incinerator
l'	**inquinamento acustico**	noise pollution
un	**oceano**	ocean
un	**OGM (organismo geneticamente modificato)**	GMO
i	**prodotti chimici**	chemicals
il	**prodotto**	product
il	**ricercatore**	researcher
il	**riciclaggio**	recycling
il	**riscaldamento globale**	global warming
gli	**scienziati**	scientists
lo	**strato di ozono**	ozone layer
lo	**sviluppo sostenibile**	sustainable development
l'	**universo**	universe

USEFUL PHRASES

ha molto rispetto per l'ambiente he's/she's very environmentally-minded
un prodotto ecologico an eco-friendly product
in futuro in the future
distruggere to destroy
inquinare to pollute; **contaminare** to contaminate
vietare to ban
salvare to save
riciclare to recycle
verde green

USEFUL WORDS *(feminine)*

le **acque di scolo**	sewage
la **bomboletta**	aerosol
la **catastrofe**	disaster
la **chiazza di petrolio**	oil slick
la **contaminazione**	contamination
la **crisi** *(pl inv)*	crisis
la **discarica** *(pl* **-che***)*	dumping ground
l' **energia eolica**	wind power
l' **energia nucleare**	nuclear power
l' **energia rinnovabile**	renewable energy
la **foresta pluviale**	rainforest
la **luna**	moon
la **marmitta catalitica**	catalytic converter
la **pioggia acida**	acid rain
la **popolazione**	population
la **raccolta differenziata (dei rifiuti)**	separate collection of household waste
le **scorie nucleari/ industriali**	nuclear/industrial waste
la **soluzione**	solution

USEFUL PHRASES

biodegradabile biodegradable
ibrido(a) hybrid
dannoso(a) per l'ambiente harmful to the environment
biologico(a) organic; biological
ecologico(a) environment-friendly
benzina senza piombo unleaded petrol
le specie in via di estinzione endangered species

ESSENTIAL WORDS *(masculine)*

gli	**adulti**	adults
il	**bambino**	child; baby; little boy
il	**cognome**	surname
il	**cognome da ragazza**	maiden name
il	**cugino**	cousin
l'	**età** *(pl inv)*	age
il	**fidanzato**	fiancé
il	**figlio**	son
il	**fratello**	brother
i	**genitori**	parents
il	**giovane**	youth, young man
i	**giovani**	young people
i	**grandi**	grown-ups
il	**marito**	husband
il	**nome**	name
il	**nome (di battesimo)**	first *or* Christian name
i	**nonni**	grandparents
il	**nonno**	grandfather
il	**padre**	father
il	**papà** *(pl inv)*	daddy
il	**parente**	relative
il	**ragazzo**	boy; boyfriend
un	**uomo** *(pl* **uomini**)	man
lo	**zio** *(pl* **zii**)	uncle

USEFUL PHRASES

quanti anni hai (*or* ha)? how old are you?
ho 15 anni – ha 40 anni I'm 15 – he/she is 40
come ti chiami (*or* si chiama)? what is your name?
mi chiamo Daniela my name is Daniela
si chiama Paolo his name is Paolo
fidanzato(a) engaged; **sposato(a)** married
divorziato(a) divorced; **separato(a)** separated
sposarsi con qn to marry sb
sposarsi to get married; **divorziare** to get divorced

ESSENTIAL WORDS *(feminine)*

la **bambina**	child; baby girl; little girl
la **cugina**	cousin
la **donna**	woman
la **famiglia**	family
la **fidanzata**	fiancée
la **figlia**	daughter
la **gente**	people
la **gioventù**	youth
la **madre**	mother
la **mamma**	mummy
la **moglie**	wife
la **nonna**	grandmother
la **persona**	person
la **ragazza**	girl; girlfriend
la **signora**	lady
la **sorella**	sister
la **zia**	aunt

USEFUL PHRASES

più giovane/vecchio(a) di me younger/older than me
hai (*or* ha) fratelli o sorelle? do you have any brothers or sisters?
ho un fratello e una sorella I have one brother and one sister
non ho fratelli I don't have any brothers or sisters
sono figlio(a) unico(a) I am an only child
tutta la famiglia the whole family
crescere to grow
invecchiare, diventare vecchio(a) to get old
vado d'accordo con i miei genitori I get on well with my parents
mia madre lavora my mother works

IMPORTANT WORDS *(masculine)*

un	**adolescente**	teenager
un	**assegno familiare**	child benefit
il	**bimbo**	child; baby; little boy
il	**neonato**	newborn baby
i	**nipoti**	grandchildren; nieces and nephews
il	**nipote**	grandson; nephew
il	**patrigno**	stepfather
lo	**scapolo**	bachelor
il	**single** *(pl inv)*	single man
il	**suocero**	father-in-law
il	**vedovo**	widower
il	**vicino**	neighbour

USEFUL WORDS *(masculine)*

il	**cognato**	brother-in-law
il	**figliastro**	stepson
il	**figlioccio**	godson
il	**fratellastro**	stepbrother
i	**gemelli**	twins
il	**genero**	son-in-law
un	**orfano**	orphan
il	**padrino**	godfather
il	**pensionato**	pensioner
il	**soprannome**	nickname
gli	**sposi novelli**	newlyweds
lo	**sposo**	bridegroom
un	**uomo anziano** *(pl* **uomini -i***)*	old man
il	**vecchio**	old man

USEFUL PHRASES

nascere to be born; **vivere** to live; **morire** to die
sono nato nel 1990 I was born in 1990
mia nonna è morta my grandmother is dead
è morta nel 1995 she died in 1995

IMPORTANT WORDS *(feminine)*

un'	**adolescente**	teenager
la	**bimba**	child; baby girl; little girl
la	**matrigna**	stepmother
la	**neonata**	newborn baby
la	**nipote**	granddaughter; niece
la	**ragazza alla pari**	au pair girl
la	**ragazza madre**	single mother
la	**single** *(pl inv)*	single woman
la	**suocera**	mother-in-law
la	**vedova**	widow
la	**vicina**	neighbour

USEFUL WORDS *(feminine)*

la	**baby sitter** *(pl inv)*	baby sitter; nanny
la	**casalinga** *(pl* **-ghe***)*	housewife
la	**cognata**	sister-in-law
la	**coppia**	couple
la	**donna anziana**	old woman
la	**figliastra**	stepdaughter
la	**figlioccia** *(pl* **-ce***)*	goddaughter
le	**gemelle**	twins
la	**madrina**	godmother
la	**nuora**	daughter-in-law
un'	**orfana**	orphan
la	**pensionata**	pensioner
la	**persona anziana**	old person
la	**sorellastra**	stepsister
la	**sposa**	bride
la	**vecchia**	old woman
la	**vecchiaia**	old age

USEFUL PHRASES

è single he/she is single
è vedovo he is a widower; **è vedova** she is a widow
sono la più giovane I am the youngest; **sono la più vecchia** I am the eldest
la mia sorella maggiore my older sister
adottare un bambino to adopt a child
prendere un bambino in affidamento to foster a child

ESSENTIAL WORDS *(masculine)*

un	**agricoltore**	farmer *(cultivating crops)*
un	**allevatore**	farmer *(raising animals)*
un	**animale**	animal
il	**bosco** *(pl* **-chi***)*	woods; forest
il	**bue** *(pl* **buoi***)*	ox
il	**campo**	field
il	**cancello**	gate
il	**cane**	dog
il	**cane pastore**	sheepdog
il	**capretto**	kid
il	**cavallo**	horse
il	**contadino**	farmer *(cultivating crops)*
il	**furgone**	van
il	**gatto**	cat
il	**maiale**	pig
il	**paese**	village
il	**pollo**	chicken
il	**tacchino**	turkey
il	**vitello**	calf

IMPORTANT WORDS *(masculine)*

un	**agnello**	lamb
il	**fattore**	farmer
il	**gallo**	cock
il	**trattore**	tractor

USEFUL PHRASES

un campo di grano a cornfield
l'agricoltura biologica organic farming
polli ruspanti free range chickens
uova di galline da cortile free range eggs
badare agli animali to look after the animals
raccogliere to harvest
raccogliere frutta/il grano to harvest fruit/grain

ESSENTIAL WORDS *(feminine)*

un'	**anatra**	duck
la	**campagna**	country
la	**cavalla**	mare
la	**contadina**	farmer *(crops)*
la	**fattoria**	farm; farmhouse
la	**gallina**	hen
la	**mucca** *(pl* **-che***)*	cow
la	**pecora**	sheep; ewe
la	**scrofa**	sow
la	**serra**	greenhouse
la	**terra**	ground; soil; earth
la	**vacca** *(pl* **-che***)*	cow

IMPORTANT WORDS *(feminine)*

la	**collina**	hill
la	**forca** *(pl* **-che***)*	fork
la	**vanga** *(pl* **-ghe***)*	spade
la	**zappa**	hoe

USEFUL PHRASES

vivere in campagna to live in the country
lavorare in una fattoria to work on a farm
raccogliere il fieno to make hay

USEFUL WORDS *(masculine)*

un	**allevamento**	farm *(with livestock)*
un	**aratro**	plough
un	**ariete**	ram
un	**asino**	donkey
il	**bestiame**	cattle
il	**capanno**	shed
il	**carro**	cart
il	**cereale**	cereal
il	**concime**	manure; fertilizer
il	**covone**	haystack
il	**fango**	mud
il	**fertilizzante**	fertilizer
il	**fienile**	hayloft
il	**fieno**	hay
il	**fossato**	ditch
il	**granaio**	barn
il	**grano**	corn; wheat
il	**gregge**	flock *(sheep)*
il	**letame**	manure
il	**mais**	maize
il	**mercato**	market
il	**montone**	ram
il	**mulino (a vento)**	(wind)mill
l'	**orzo**	barley
il	**paesaggio**	landscape
il	**pastore**	shepherd
il	**pollaio**	henhouse
il	**porcile**	pigsty
il	**pulcino**	chick
il	**puledro**	foal
il	**raccolto**	crop; harvest
il	**seme**	seed
il	**solco** *(pl* **-chi***)*	furrow
lo	**spaventapasseri** *(pl inv)*	scarecrow
lo	**stagno**	pond
il	**suolo**	ground, soil
il	**toro**	bull
il	**vino**	vine

USEFUL WORDS *(feminine)*

un'	**aia**	farmyard
l'	**avena**	oats
la	**brughiera**	moor, heath
la	**capra**	goat
la	**capretta**	kid
la	**falce**	sickle
la	**lana**	wool
la	**mandria**	herd *(cattle)*
la	**mietitrebbia**	combine harvester
un'	**oca** *(pl* **-che***)*	goose
la	**paglia**	straw
la	**scala**	ladder
la	**segale**	rye
la	**stalla**	cow shed; stable
l'	**uva**	grapes
la	**vendemmia**	grape harvest, grape picking

USEFUL PHRASES

coltivare to grow *(crops etc)*
mungere una vacca to milk a cow
macellare to slaughter *(animal)*

fish and insects

ESSENTIAL WORDS *(masculine)*

i	**frutti di mare**	seafood
il	**pesce**	fish
il	**pesce rosso**	goldfish

IMPORTANT WORDS *(masculine)*

il	**granchio**	crab
un	**insetto**	insect

USEFUL WORDS *(masculine)*

un	**acquario**	aquarium
il	**baco da seta**	silkworm
il	**bruco** *(pl* **-chi***)*	caterpillar
il	**calabrone**	hornet
il	**calamaro**	squid
un	**eglefino**	haddock
il	**gambero**	shrimp
il	**gambero d'acqua dolce**	crayfish
il	**girino**	tadpole
il	**grillo**	cricket
il	**luccio**	pike
il	**merluzzo**	cod
il	**moscerino**	midge
il	**polpo**	octopus
il	**ragno**	spider
il	**salmone**	salmon
gli	**scampi**	scampi
lo	**scarafaggio**	cockroach
lo	**squalo**	shark
il	**tonno**	tuna
il	**verme**	worm

USEFUL PHRASES

nuotare to swim
volare to fly
stiamo andando a pescare we're going fishing

ESSENTIAL WORDS *(feminine)*

l' **acqua**	water

IMPORTANT WORDS *(feminine)*

la **mosca** *(pl* **-che***)*	fly
la **sardina**	sardine
la **trota**	trout

USEFUL WORDS *(feminine)*

un' **ala**	wing
un' **allergia**	allergy
un' **anguilla**	eel
un' **ape**	bee
un' **aragosta**	lobster
un' **aringa** *(pl* **-ghe***)*	herring
la **cavalletta**	grasshopper
la **cicala**	cicada
la **cimice**	bed bug
la **coccinella**	ladybird
la **cozza**	mussel
la **falena**	moth
la **farfalla**	butterfly
la **formica** *(pl* **-che***)*	ant
la **libellula**	dragonfly
la **medusa**	jellyfish
un' **ostrica** *(pl* **-che***)*	oyster
la **pulce**	flea
la **rana**	frog
la **sogliola**	sole
la **tarma**	moth *(clothes)*
la **vespa**	wasp
la **zanzara**	mosquito

USEFUL PHRASES

una puntura di vespa a wasp sting
una ragnatela a spider's web

ESSENTIAL WORDS *(masculine)*

l'	**aceto**	vinegar
gli	**antipasti**	starters
un	**aperitivo**	aperitif
un	**arrosto**	roast
il	**bar** *(pl inv)*	café-bar
il	**bicchiere**	glass
il	**brodo**	(clear) soup, bouillon
il	**burro**	butter
il	**caffè** *(pl inv)*	coffee; café
il	**caffelatte** *(pl inv)*	coffee with milk
il	**cameriere**	waiter
i	**cereali**	cereal
il	**cibo**	food
il	**cibo in scatola**	tinned food
il	**coltello**	knife
il	**conto**	bill
il	**croissant** *(pl inv)*	croissant
il	**cucchiaino**	teaspoon
il	**cucchiaio**	spoon
il	**cuoco** *(pl* **-chi**)	cook
il	**dessert** *(pl inv)*	dessert
il	**dolce**	sweet, dessert
il	**filetto**	steak
il	**filoncino**	French stick
il	**formaggio**	cheese
i	**frutti di mare**	seafood
il	**frutto** *(pl f* **frutta**)	piece of fruit
il	**gelato**	ice cream
un	**hamburger** *(pl inv)*	hamburger
il	**latte**	milk
il	**litro**	litre
il	**maiale**	pork
il	**menù** *(pl inv)*	menu
il	**menù a prezzo fisso**	fixed-price menu
l'	**olio**	oil
il	**pane**	bread
il	**pane tostato**	toast
il	**panino**	bread roll; sandwich

ESSENTIAL WORDS *(feminine)*

l' **acqua (minerale)**	(mineral) water
la **bibita**	soft drink
la **birra**	beer
la **birra alla spina**	draught beer
la **bistecca** (*pl* **-che**)	steak
la **bottiglia**	bottle
le **caramelle**	sweets
la **carne**	meat
la **carne di manzo**	beef
la **cena**	dinner
la **cioccolata (calda)**	(hot) chocolate
la **Coca Cola®** (*pl* **-che -e**)	Coke®
la **colazione**	breakfast
la **crêpe** (*pl inv*)	pancake
un' **entrecôte** (*pl inv*)	(entrecôte) steak
la **fame**	hunger
la **fetta**	slice
la **forchetta**	fork
la **frutta**	fruit
un' **insalata**	salad
un' **insalata mista**	mixed salad
la **lattina**	can
la **limonata**	lemonade
la **marmellata**	jam
la **marmellata d'arance**	marmalade
la **minestra**	soup
un' **oliva**	olive
un' **omelette** (*pl inv*)	omelette
la **pasta**	pastry; small cake
la **pasticceria**	cake shop
le **patatine**	crisps
le **patatine fritte**	chips, fries
la **pescheria**	fish shop
la **salsiccia** (*pl* **-ce**)	sausage
la **scatola**	tin, can; box
la **sete**	thirst
le **stoviglie**	dishes

ESSENTIAL WORDS *(masculine continued)*

il **pasto pronto**	ready-made meal
il **pesce**	fish
il **piatto**	plate; dish; course
il **piatto del giorno**	today's special
il **picnic** *(pl inv)*	picnic
il **pollo (arrosto)**	(roast) chicken
il **pranzo**	lunch
il **primo (piatto)**	first course
il **prosciutto**	ham
il **prosciutto cotto**	cooked ham
il **prosciutto crudo**	cured ham
un **quarto**	quarter *(bottle/litre etc)*
il **riso**	rice
il **ristorante**	restaurant
il **salame**	salami
il **sale**	salt
il **secondo (piatto)**	main course
il **servizio**	service
il **succo di frutta**	fruit juice
il **tè** *(pl inv)*	tea
il **toast** *(pl inv)*	toasted sandwich
un **uovo** *(pl f* **uova***)*	egg
un **uovo alla coque**	soft-boiled egg
un **uovo sodo**	hard-boiled egg
il **vino**	wine
il **vitello**	veal
lo **yogurt** *(pl inv)*	yoghurt
lo **zucchero**	sugar

USEFUL PHRASES

cucinare to cook; **mangiare** to eat
bere to drink; **inghiottire** to swallow
il mio piatto preferito my favourite dish
cosa vuoi da bere? what are you having to drink?
è buono it's nice
avere fame, essere affamato(a) to be hungry
avere sete, essere assetato(a) to be thirsty

ESSENTIAL WORDS *(feminine continued)*

la **tavola**	table
la **tazza**	cup
la **torta**	cake
la **trattoria**	restaurant
le **uova**	eggs
le **verdure**	vegetables
la **zuppa**	soup

IMPORTANT WORDS *(feminine)*

la **brocca** *(pl* **-che***)*	jug
la **cameriera**	waitress
la **capocuoca** *(pl* **-che***)*	chef
la **caraffa**	carafe
la **carne alla griglia**	grilled meat
la **carne macinata**	mince
la **cotoletta di maiale**	pork chop
la **crostata**	tart
la **cuoca** *(pl* **-che***)*	cook
la **farina**	flour
le **lumache**	snails
la **maionese**	mayonnaise
la **mancia** *(pl* **-ce***)*	tip
la **mensa**	canteen
la **merendina**	snack
la **panna**	cream
la **pizza**	pizza
la **ricetta**	recipe
la **scelta**	choice
la **scodella**	bowl
la **senape**	mustard
la **teiera**	teapot
la **vaniglia**	vanilla

IMPORTANT WORDS *(masculine)*

l'	**aglio**	garlic
un	**agnello**	lamb
il	**bricco** *(pl* **-chi***)* **del latte**	milk jug
il	**capocuoco** *(pl* **-chi***)*	chef
il	**carrello**	trolley
lo	**chef** *(pl inv)*	chef
il	**commercio equo e solidale**	fair trade
il	**coniglio**	rabbit
il	**coperto**	cover charge; place setting
il	**cordiale**	cordial
il	**cucchiaio da portata**	tablespoon
il	**digestivo**	after-dinner liqueur
il	**gusto**	taste; flavour
il	**montone**	mutton
un	**odore**	smell
il	**peperone**	bell pepper
il	**prezzo fisso**	set price
il	**prezzo tutto compreso**	inclusive price
il	**sapore**	flavour
lo	**sciroppo**	syrup
lo	**spuntino**	snack, bite to eat
il	**supplemento**	extra charge
il	**vitello**	veal

USEFUL WORDS *(masculine)*

l'	**apribottiglie** *(pl inv)*	bottle opener
un	**apriscatole** *(pl inv)*	tin opener
il	**brandy** *(pl inv)*	brandy
il	**cacao**	cocoa
il	**cavatappi** *(pl inv)*	corkscrew
lo	**champagne** *(pl inv)*	champagne
il	**cibo**	food
il	**cubetto di ghiaccio**	ice cube
il	**fegato**	liver
il	**ketchup** *(pl inv)*	ketchup
il	**miele**	honey
il	**panettone**	cake eaten at Christmas

USEFUL WORDS *(feminine)*

la **briciola**	crumb
la **cannuccia** *(pl* **-ce***)*	straw
la **carta dei vini**	wine list
la **cotoletta**	chop
le **cozze**	mussels
la **crema**	custard
la **fetta di pane tostato**	Melba toast
la **gelatina**	jelly
la **limonata**	freshly-squeezed lemon juice
la **margarina**	margarine
la **pancetta**	bacon
la **panna montata**	whipped cream
la **panna per cucina**	cream for cooking
la **pasta**	pasta
la **pasta in bianco**	plain pasta *(with butter/oil)*
la **pasta in brodo**	pasta in broth
la **pastasciutta**	pasta in a sauce
la **roba da mangiare**	food
la **salsa**	sauce
la **selvaggina**	game
la **tisana**	herbal tea
la **tovaglia**	tablecloth
la **trippa**	tripe

USEFUL PHRASES

lavare i piatti to do the dishes
quando torniamo da scuola facciamo merenda we have a snack when we come back from school
fare colazione to have breakfast
delizioso(a) delicious; **disgustoso(a)** disgusting
buon appetito! enjoy your meal!; **salute!** cheers!
il conto, per favore! the bill please!
"il servizio non è compreso" "service not included"
mangiare fuori to eat out
invitare qn a pranzo to invite sb to lunch
prendere qualcosa da bere to have drinks

USEFUL WORDS *(masculine continued)*

il **panino dolce**	sweet bun
il **parmigiano**	parmesan cheese
il **pasticcino**	petit four; fancy cake
il **pasto**	meal
il **pâté** *(pl inv)*	pâté
il **pesto**	pesto sauce
il **piattino**	saucer
il **pollame**	poultry
il **proprietario**	owner
il **puré di patate**	mashed potatoes
il **risotto**	risotto
il **roastbeef** *(pl inv)*	roast beef
il **rognone**	kidneys
il **sandwich** *(pl inv)*	sandwich
il **self-service** *(pl inv)*	self-service restaurant
il **sidro**	cider
lo **spiedino**	kebab; skewer
lo **stufato**	stew
il **sugo** *(pl* **-ghi***)* **di carne**	gravy
il **tappo**	cork
il **thermos** *(pl inv)*	flask
il **tovagliolo**	napkin
il **vassoio**	tray
il **whisky** *(pl inv)*	whisky

USEFUL PHRASES

apparecchiare la tavola to set the table
sparecchiare la tavola to clear the table
pranzare to have lunch
cenare to have dinner
assaggiare qc to taste sth
che buon profumo! that smells good!
vino bianco/rosso/rosato white/red wine/rosé
una bistecca al sangue/a media cottura/ben cotta a rare/medium/ well-done steak
un toast con formaggio e prosciutto a ham and cheese toastie

SMOKING

un	**accendino**	lighter
il	**cerino**	match *(made of wax)*
il	**fiammifero**	match
il	**fumatore**	smoker
la	**fumatrice**	smoker
il	**pacchetto di sigarette**	packet of cigarettes
la	**pipa**	pipe
il	**portacenere** *(pl inv)*	ashtray
la	**sigaretta**	cigarette
il	**sigaro**	cigar
il	**tabaccaio**	tobacconist's
il	**tabacco**	tobacco

USEFUL PHRASES

una scatola di fiammiferi a box of matches
hai (*or* **ha) da accendere?** do you have a light?
accendere una sigaretta to light up
"vietato fumare" "no smoking"
non fumo I don't smoke
ho smesso di fumare I've stopped smoking
fumare fa molto male alla salute smoking is very bad for you

ESSENTIAL WORDS *(masculine)*

un	**amico** *(pl* **-ci***)* **di penna**	pen friend
il	**ballo**	dance
il	**biglietto**	ticket
il	**calcetto**	table football
il	**cantante**	singer
il	**canto**	singing
il	**CD** *(pl inv)*	CD
il	**cellulare**	mobile phone
il	**cinema** *(pl inv)*	cinema
il	**concerto**	concert
il	**decoder** *(pl inv)*	digibox
il	**dépliant** *(pl inv)*	leaflet
il	**disco** *(pl* **-chi***)*	record
il	**divertimento**	entertainment; pastime
il	**DVD** *(pl inv)*	DVD
il	**film** *(pl inv)*	film *(movie)*
il	**fine settimana** *(pl inv)*	weekend
il	**fumetto**	comic strip
il	**gioco** *(pl* **-chi***)*	game
il	**giornale**	newspaper
un	**hobby** *(pl inv)*	hobby
	Internet	internet
un	**iPod®** *(pl inv)*	iPod
il	**lettore CD/DVD/MP3**	CD/DVD/MP3 player
il	**museo**	museum; art gallery
il	**passatempo**	hobby
il	**programma**	programme
il	**romanzo**	novel
il	**romanzo giallo**	detective novel
gli	**scacchi**	chess
lo	**schermo al plasma**	plasma screen
il	**socio**	member *(of club)*
lo	**spettacolo**	show
lo	**sport** *(pl inv)*	sport
il	**teatro**	theatre
il	**telegiornale**	TV news
il	**tempo libero**	free time
il	**videogioco** *(pl* **-chi***)*	video game

ESSENTIAL WORDS *(feminine)*

un'	**amica** *(pl* **-che***)* **di penna**	pen friend
un'	**antenna parabolica** *(pl* **-e -che***)*	satellite dish
la	**cantante**	singer
la	**canzone**	song
le	**carte da gioco**	cards
la	**console per videogiochi** *(pl inv)*	games console
la	**discoteca** *(pl* **-che***)*	disco; night club
un'	**escursione**	trip; outing; hike
la	**festa**	party
la	**foto** *(pl inv)*	photo
la	**lettura**	reading
la	**macchina fotografica** *(pl* **-e -che***)*	camera
la	**musica (pop/classica)**	(pop/classical) music
la	**paghetta**	pocket money
la	**passeggiata**	walk
la	**pellicola**	film *(for camera)*
la	**pista di pattinaggio**	skating rink
la	**pubblicità** *(pl inv)*	publicity; advert
la	**radio** *(pl inv)*	radio
la	**rivista**	magazine
la	**stampa**	the press
la	**star** *(m+f pl inv)*	film star
la	**televisione**	television
la	**TV** *(pl inv)*	TV
la	**TV satellitare**	satellite TV

USEFUL PHRASES

esco con i miei amici I go out with my friends
leggo il giornale I read the newspaper
guardo la televisione I watch television
gioco a calcio/tennis/carte I play football/tennis/cards
fare bricolage to do DIY
fare il/la baby sitter to baby-sit
fare zapping to channel-hop
andare in discoteca to go clubbing

IMPORTANT WORDS *(masculine)*

gli	**annunci (sul giornale)**	adverts; small ads
il	**cartone animato**	cartoon
il	**computer** *(pl inv)*	computer
il	**concorso**	competition
il	**disegno**	drawing
il	**giocattolo**	toy
un	**incontro**	meeting
un	**manifesto**	notice; poster
il	**masterizzatore CD/DVD**	CD/DVD writer
il	**messaggino**	text message
il	**PC** *(pl inv)*	PC
il	**quadro**	painting
il	**ragazzo**	boy; boyfriend
il	**sito web**	website
un	**sms** *(pl inv)*	text message

USEFUL WORDS *(masculine)*

il	**blog** *(pl inv)*	blog
il	**campeggio**	campsite; holiday camp
il	**coro**	choir
il	**cruciverba** *(pl inv)*	crossword puzzle(s)
il	**fan** *(pl inv)*	fan
il	**gioco** *(pl* **-chi***)* **da tavolo**	board game
il	**monopattino**	scooter
il	**night club** *(pl inv)*	night club
i	**pattini in linea**	rollerblades
lo	**scout** *(pl inv)*	scout
lo	**skateboard** *(pl inv)*	skateboard

USEFUL PHRASES

emozionante exciting
noioso(a) boring
divertente funny
lavorare a maglia to knit
cucire to sew

IMPORTANT WORDS *(feminine)*

la **collezione**	collection
la **macchina fotografica digitale**	digital camera
la **mostra**	exhibition
la **notte**	evening; night
la **pittura**	painting
la **ragazza**	girl; girlfriend
la **sera**	evening
la **serie televisiva**	serial
la **telenovela** *(pl inv)*	soap (opera)
la **videocamera**	camcorder

USEFUL WORDS *(feminine)*

la **chat** *(pl inv)*	chat; chatroom
la **diapositiva**	slide
la **fan** *(pl inv)*	fan
la **fotografia**	photograph; photography
la **hit parade** *(pl inv)*	charts
le **parole crociate**	crossword puzzle(s)
la **scout** *(pl inv)*	girl scout

USEFUL PHRASES

non è male it's not bad
abbastanza bello(a) quite good
ballare to dance
fare fotografie to take photos
mi annoio I'm bored
ci vediamo di venerdì we meet on Fridays
sto risparmiando per comprare un lettore DVD I'm saving up to buy a DVD recorder
mi piacerebbe fare il giro del mondo I'd like to go round the world

ESSENTIAL WORDS *(masculine)*

un	**ananas** *(pl inv)*	pineapple
il	**frutto** *(pl f* **frutta**)	(piece of) fruit
il	**lampone**	raspberry
il	**limone**	lemon
il	**pomodoro**	tomato
il	**pompelmo**	grapefruit

IMPORTANT WORDS *(masculine)*

un	**albero da frutta**	fruit tree
il	**melone**	melon

USEFUL WORDS *(masculine)*

un	**avocado** *(pl inv)*	avocado
il	**dattero**	date
il	**fico** *(pl* **-chi**)	fig
il	**kiwi** *(pl inv)*	kiwi fruit
il	**mandarino**	tangerine
il	**mirtillo**	blueberry
il	**nocciolo**	stone *(in fruit)*
il	**rabarbaro**	rhubarb
il	**ribes** *(pl inv)* **nero**	blackcurrant
il	**ribes** *(pl inv)* **rosso**	redcurrant
il	**semino**	pip *(in fruit)*

USEFUL PHRASES

maturo(a) ripe
acerbo(a) unripe
un chilo di a kilo of
mezzo chilo di half a kilo of
un cestino di lamponi a punnet of raspberries

ESSENTIAL WORDS *(feminine)*

un'	**albicocca** *(pl* **-che***)*	apricot
un'	**arancia** *(pl* **-ce***)*	orange
la	**banana**	banana
la	**buccia** *(pl* **-ce***)*	skin
la	**caldarrosta**	(roasted) chestnut
la	**castagna**	chestnut
la	**ciliegia** *(pl* **-ge***)*	cherry
la	**fragola**	strawberry
la	**frutta**	fruit
la	**mela**	apple
la	**pera**	pear
la	**pesca** *(pl* **-che***)*	peach
la	**pescanoce**	nectarine
l'	**uva**	grapes
l'	**uvetta**	raisin

USEFUL WORDS *(feminine)*

un'	**arachide**	peanut
la	**bacca** *(pl* **-che***)*	berry
la	**melagrana**	pomegranate
la	**mora**	blackberry
la	**nocciola**	hazelnut
la	**noce**	walnut
la	**noce di anacardo**	cashew nut
la	**noce di cocco**	coconut
la	**prugna**	plum
la	**prugna secca** *(pl* **-e -che***)*	prune
l'	**uva spina**	gooseberry
la	**vite**	vine

USEFUL PHRASES

un succo d'arancia/d'ananas an orange/a pineapple juice
un grappolo d'uva a bunch of grapes
sbucciare un frutto to peel a fruit
scivolare su una buccia di banana to slip on a banana skin

furniture and appliances

ESSENTIAL WORDS *(masculine)*

un **armadietto**	cupboard
un **armadio**	wardrobe
il **calorifero**	radiator
il **congelatore**	freezer
il **fornello (elettrico/a gas)**	(electric/gas) cooker
il **frigo** *(pl* **-ghi***)*	fridge
il **frigorifero**	refrigerator
il **guardaroba** *(pl inv)*	wardrobe
il **letto**	bed
il **mobile**	piece of furniture
i **mobili**	furniture
un **orologio**	clock
il **paralume** *(pl inv)*	lampshade
lo **scaffale**	shelf
lo **specchio**	mirror
il **tavolo**	table
il **telefono**	telephone
il **telefono fisso**	landline

IMPORTANT WORDS *(masculine)*

il **baule**	chest
il **bollitore**	kettle
il **cellulare**	mobile phone
il **divano**	sofa
un **elettrodomestico**	domestic appliance
un **ereader** *(pl inv)*	e-reader
il **ferro da stiro**	iron
il **forno a microonde**	microwave oven
il **lettore di CD/DVD**	CD/DVD player
il **lettore MP3**	MP3 player
il **libro elettronico**	e-book
il **monolocale**	studio flat
il **piano**	piano
il **quadro**	painting, picture
il **tablet** *(pl inv)*	tablet
il **tavolino**	coffee table
il **telefono cordless**	cordless phone

ESSENTIAL WORDS *(feminine)*

la **lampada**	lamp
la **lavastoviglie** *(pl inv)*	dishwasher
la **lavatrice**	washing machine
la **poltrona**	armchair
la **radio** *(pl inv)*	radio
la **radiosveglia**	radio alarm
la **sedia**	chair
la **stanza**	room
la **stufa**	heater
la **tavola**	table
la **televisione**	television

IMPORTANT WORDS *(feminine)*

un' **asciugatrice**	tumble-dryer
un' **aspirapolvere** *(pl inv)*	vacuum cleaner
la **credenza**	sideboard
la **libreria**	bookcase
la **radio digitale**	digital radio
la **scrivania**	(writing) desk

furniture and appliances

USEFUL WORDS *(masculine)*

un	**addetto ai traslochi**	removal man
un	**altoparlante**	loudspeaker
un	**asciugacapelli** *(pl inv)*	hairdryer
il	**camion dei traslochi** *(pl inv)*	removal van
il	**caricabatterie**	charger
il	**carrello**	trolley
il	**cassetto**	drawer
il	**cassettone**	chest of drawers
il	**comodino**	bedside table
il	**computer** *(pl inv)*	computer
il	**forno**	oven
i	**letti a castello**	bunk beds
il	**lettino**	cot
il	**letto a una piazza**	single bed
il	**letto matrimoniale**	double bed
il	**materasso**	mattress
i	**mobili**	furniture
il	**navigatore satellitare**	sat nav
il	**portaombrelli** *(pl inv)*	umbrella stand
lo	**sgabello**	stool
lo	**stereo compatto**	music centre
il	**tappeto**	rug
il	**telecomando**	remote control
il	**trasloco**	move
il	**tritatutto** *(pl inv)*	food processor

USEFUL PHRASES

un appartamento ammobiliato a furnished flat
accendere/spegnere la stufa to switch the heater on/off
ho rifatto il mio letto I've made my bed
sedersi to sit down
mettere qc in forno to put sth in the oven
tirare le tende to draw the curtains
chiudere le imposte to close the shutters

USEFUL WORDS *(feminine)*

un'	**antenna**	aerial
un'	**antenna parabolica** (*pl* **-e -che**)	satellite dish
la	**bilancia** (*pl* **-ce**)	scales
la	**cornice**	frame
la	**culla**	cradle
le	**imposte**	shutters
la	**lampada a stelo**	standard lamp
la	**lampada alogena**	halogen lamp
la	**macchina per cucire**	sewing machine
la	**moquette**	fitted carpet
la	**pennetta USB**	USB stick
la	**piantana**	standard lamp
la	**piastra per capelli**	hair straighteners
la	**scala a libretto**	step ladder
la	**segreteria telefonica** (*pl* **-e -che**)	answering machine
la	**tapparella**	blind
la	**tavola da stiro**	ironing board
la	**toilette**	toilet; dressing table
la	**TV a schermo panoramico**	widescreen TV
la	**videocamera**	camcorder

USEFUL PHRASES

è un appartamento di 4 stanze it's a 4-roomed flat
la colazione/la cena è pronta! breakfast/dinner is ready!
il pranzo è pronto! lunch is ready!

ESSENTIAL WORDS

le	**Alpi**	the Alps
gli	**Appennini**	Apennines
l'	**Atlantico**	the Atlantic
	Bruxelles	Brussels
la	**Costa Azzurra**	Côte d'Azur
le	**Dolomiti**	Dolomites
l'	**est** *(m)*	the east
l'	**estero** *(m)*	foreign countries; abroad
	Firenze	Florence
la	**Germania**	Germany
	Genova	Genoa
	Livorno	Leghorn
la	**Lombardia**	Lombardy
	Londra	London
	Marsiglia	Marseilles
il	**Mediterraneo**	the Mediterranean
il	**Meridione**	the South
	Milano	Milan
la	**montagna**	mountain
il	**Monte Bianco**	Mont Blanc
	Napoli	Naples
il	**nord**	the north
l'	**ovest** *(m)*	the west
	Parigi	Paris
il	**passo**	pass *(mountain)*
il	**Piemonte**	Piedmont
	Roma	Rome
la	**Sardegna**	Sardinia
la	**Sicilia**	Sicily
il	**sud**	the south
il	**Tevere**	the Tiber
	Torino	Turin
la	**Toscana**	Tuscany
il	**Vaticano**	the Vatican
	Venezia	Venice

IMPORTANT WORDS

	Edimburgo *(f)*	Edinburgh
il	**Tamigi**	the Thames

USEFUL WORDS

	Atene	Athens
	Berlino	Berlin
il	**canale della Manica, la Manica**	English Channel
la	**capitale**	capital
l'	**Estremo Oriente**	the Far East
	Ginevra	Geneva
le	**isole britanniche**	the British Isles
	L'Aia	The Hague
	Lisbona	Lisbon
il	**Medio Oriente**	the Middle East
	Mosca	Moscow
il	**Pacifico**	Pacific
	Pechino	Beijing
il	**Polo Nord/Sud**	the North/South Pole
la	**provincia** *(pl* **-ce***)*	province
	Varsavia	Warsaw

USEFUL PHRASES

andare a Londra/Roma to go to London/Rome
andare in Lombardia to go to Lombardy
vengo da Milano/dal sud I come from Milan/from the south
all'estero abroad

a nord in *or* to the north
a sud in *or* to the south
a est in *or* to the east
a ovest in *or* to the west

l'Italia del sud *or* **meridionale** southern Italy
l'Italia del nord *or* **settentrionale** northern Italy

GREETINGS

ciao hello, hi; bye
come stai (*or* sta)? how are you?
come va? how are you?
bene fine *(in reply)*
piacere (di conoscerla) pleased to meet you
pronto hello *(on telephone)*
buonasera good afternoon; good evening
buonanotte good night
arrivederci goodbye
ci vediamo domani see you tomorrow
ci vediamo più tardi see you later

BEST WISHES

buon compleanno happy birthday
buon Natale merry Christmas
felice anno nuovo *or* **buon anno** happy New Year
buona Pasqua happy Easter
saluti best wishes
auguri best wishes
benvenuto(a) welcome
congratulazioni congratulations
buon appetito enjoy your meal
cari saluti all the best
divertiti (*or* si diverta) enjoy yourself
buona fortuna good luck
buon viaggio safe journey
salute bless you *(after a sneeze)*; cheers
alla tua (*or* alla vostra, *etc*)**!** your health!

SURPRISE

mio Dio my goodness
cosa? what?
come? what?
capisco oh, I see
ma dai! really?
beh... well...
veramente? really?
stai scherzando? are you kidding?
che fortuna! how lucky!

POLITENESS

scusa (*or* mi scusi) I'm sorry; excuse me
per favore please
grazie thank you
no, grazie no thank you
sì, grazie yes please
di niente not at all, don't mention it, you're welcome
volentieri gladly

AGREEMENT

sì yes
naturalmente of course
d'accordo OK
va bene fine

DISAGREEMENT

no no
certo che no of course not
non esiste no way
per niente not at all
al contrario on the contrary
questa poi! well I never
che faccia tosta what a cheek
bada agli affari tuoi mind your own business

DIFFICULTIES

aiuto! help!
al fuoco! fire!
ahi! ouch!
scusa (*or* scusi) (I'm) sorry, excuse me, I beg your pardon
mi dispiace I'm sorry
che peccato what a pity
che seccatura what a nuisance
che noia how boring
sono stufo(a) I'm fed up
non lo sopporto più I can't stand it any more
mamma mia oh dear
è terribile how awful

ORDERS

attento(a) be careful
fermati (*or* si fermi) stop
ehi, tu hey, you there
fuori di qui clear off
silenzio shh
basta that's enough
vietato fumare no smoking
andiamo let's go
continua go ahead, go on

OTHERS

non ne ho idea no idea
forse perhaps, maybe
non so I don't know
posso aiutarti (*or* aiutarla)? can I help you?
eccoti qua there you are
ecco tieni (*or* tenga) here you are; take this
arrivo just coming
non preoccuparti don't worry
non ne vale la pena it's not worth it
a proposito by the way
caro(a) darling
poverino(a) poor thing
tanto meglio so much the better
non importa I don't mind; it doesn't matter
per me è lo stesso (*or* è uguale) it's all the same to me
che sfortuna too bad; bad luck!
dipende it depends
cosa devo fare? what shall I do?
a che scopo? what's the point?
mi dà fastidio it annoys me
mi dà ai nervi it gets on my nerves

ESSENTIAL WORDS *(masculine)*

un	**appuntamento**	appointment
il	**dentista**	dentist
il	**dottore**	doctor
un	**incidente**	accident
un	**infermiere**	(male) nurse
il	**letto**	bed
il	**medico**	doctor
un	**ospedale**	hospital
il	**paziente**	patient
lo	**stomaco**	stomach

IMPORTANT WORDS *(masculine)*

un	**antisettico**	antiseptic
il	**caldo**	heat
il	**cerotto**	(sticking) plaster
il	**cotone idrofilo**	cotton wool
il	**cucchiaio**	spoon; spoonful
il	**dolore**	pain
il	**farmacista**	chemist
il	**farmaco**	medicine, drug
il	**freddo**	cold
il	**gesso**	plaster cast
un	**intervento chirurgico**	operation, surgery
il	**Pronto Soccorso**	Accident and Emergency, A&E
il	**sangue**	blood
lo	**sciroppo**	syrup
lo	**studio medico**	surgery
un	**unguento**	ointment

USEFUL PHRASES

c'è stato un incidente there's been an accident
essere ricoverato(a) in ospedale to be admitted to hospital
devi (*or* **deve) stare a letto** you must stay in bed
essere malato(a) to be ill; **sentirsi meglio** to feel better
mi sono fatto male I have hurt myself
mi sono tagliato un dito I have cut my finger
mi sono slogato la caviglia I have sprained my ankle
si è rotto un braccio he has broken his arm

ESSENTIAL WORDS *(feminine)*

un'	**aspirina**	aspirin
la	**dentista**	dentist
la	**dottoressa**	doctor
la	**farmacia**	chemist's *(shop)*
la	**farmacista**	chemist, pharmacy
la	**febbre**	temperature
un'	**infermiera**	nurse
la	**pasticca** (*pl* **-che**)	tablet, pill
la	**pastiglia**	tablet, pill
la	**paziente**	patient
la	**pillola**	pill
la	**salute**	health

IMPORTANT WORDS *(feminine)*

un'	**ambulanza**	ambulance
un'	**assicurazione**	insurance
la	**barella**	stretcher
la	**clinica** (*pl* **-che**)	clinic
la	**compressa**	tablet
la	**diarrea**	diarrhoea
la	**fascia** (*pl* **-sce**)	bandage
la	**ferita**	wound
un'	**influenza**	flu
l'	**influenza suina**	swine flu
un'	**ingessatura**	plaster cast
un'	**iniezione**	injection
un'	**insolazione**	sunstroke
la	**malattia**	illness
la	**medicina**	medicine
un'	**operazione**	operation
la	**ricetta**	prescription
la	**scottatura**	burn; scald

USEFUL PHRASES

mi sono ustionato I have burnt myself
mi fa male la gola/la testa/lo stomaco I've got a sore throat/ a headache/a stomach ache
avere la febbre to have a temperature

USEFUL WORDS *(masculine)*

un	**ascesso**	abscess
un	**attacco** *(pl* **-chi***)*	fit
un	**attacco cardiaco** *(pl* **-chi -ci***)*	heart attack
i	**batteri**	germs, bacteria
il	**cancro**	cancer
il	**capogiro**	dizziness
il	**graffio**	scratch
il	**livido**	bruise
il	**mal di gola**	sore throat
il	**microbo**	germ
il	**morbillo**	measles
il	**nervo**	nerve
gli	**orecchioni**	mumps
il	**polso**	pulse
il	**preservativo**	condom
il	**ricostituente**	tonic
il	**riposo**	rest
lo	**shock** *(pl inv)*	shock
lo	**stress** *(pl inv)*	stress
lo	**svenimento**	fainting
il	**vaiolo**	smallpox
il	**veleno**	poison

USEFUL PHRASES

ho sonno I'm sleepy
ho la nausea I feel sick
dimagrire to lose weight
ingrassare to put on weight
inghiottire to swallow
sanguinare to bleed
vomitare to vomit
essere in forma to be in good shape
morire to die
riposare to rest

USEFUL WORDS *(feminine)*

l'	**appendicite**	appendicitis
l'	**AIDS**	AIDS
l'	**articolazione**	joint
la	**ASL (Azienda Sanitaria Locale)**	local heath centre
la	**cassetta del pronto soccorso**	first aid kit
la	**cicatrice**	scar
la	**dentiera**	false teeth
la	**dieta**	diet
un'	**emicrania**	migraine
un'	**epidemia**	epidemic
la	**fasciatura**	dressing
la	**febbre da fieno**	hay fever
la	**gravidanza**	pregnancy
la	**guarigione**	recovery
un'	**infiammazione**	inflammation
la	**nausea**	nausea
la	**pandemia**	pandemic
la	**pomata**	ointment
la	**radiografia**	X-ray
la	**rosolia**	German measles
la	**scheggia** (*pl* **-ge**)	splinter
la	**sedia a rotelle**	wheelchair
la	**stampella**	crutch
la	**tonsillite**	tonsillitis
la	**tosse**	cough
la	**tosse canina**	whooping cough
la	**trasfusione (di sangue)**	blood transfusion
la	**varicella**	chickenpox

USEFUL PHRASES

curare to cure; to treat; **stare meglio** to get better
gravemente ferito(a) seriously injured
sei (*or* è) assicurato(a)? are you insured?
sono raffreddato(a) I have a cold
mi fa male! that hurts!; it hurts!
respirare to breathe; **svenire** to faint; **tossire** to cough
perdere conoscenza to lose consciousness
avere il braccio al collo to have one's arm in a sling

ESSENTIAL WORDS *(masculine)*

un	**albergo** *(pl* **-ghi***)*	hotel
un	**ascensore**	lift
un	**assegno**	cheque
i	**bagagli**	luggage
il	**bagno**	bathroom
il	**balcone**	balcony
il	**bar** *(pl inv)*	bar
il	**cameriere**	waiter
il	**conto**	bill
il	**direttore**	manager
il	**facchino**	porter
un	**hotel** *(pl inv)*	hotel
i	**letti gemelli**	twin beds
il	**letto matrimoniale**	double bed
il	**modulo**	form
il	**numero**	number
un	**ospite**	guest
il	**passaporto**	passport
il	**pasto**	lunch; meal
il	**piano**	floor; storey
il	**pianoterra**	ground floor
il	**pranzo**	lunch
il	**prezzo**	price
un	**receptionist** *(pl inv)*	receptionist
il	**ristorante**	restaurant
il	**rumore**	noise
il	**soggiorno**	stay
gli	**spiccioli**	change, loose coins
il	**telefono**	telephone

USEFUL PHRASES

vorrei prenotare una camera I would like to book a room
una camera con doccia/bagno a room with a shower/bathroom
una camera singola/matrimoniale a single/double room
una camera a due letti a twin-bedded room

ESSENTIAL WORDS *(feminine)*

la	**camera**	room
la	**cameriera**	waitress; chambermaid
la	**caparra**	deposit
la	**carta di credito**	credit card
la	**chiave**	key
la	**colazione**	breakfast
la	**comodità** *(pl inv)*	comfort; convenience
la	**data**	date
la	**direttrice**	manager
la	**doccia** *(pl* **-ce***)*	shower
la	**mezza pensione**	half board
la	**notte**	night
un'	**ospite**	guest
la	**pensione**	guest house
la	**pensione completa**	full board
la	**piscina**	swimming pool
la	**reception** *(pl inv)*	reception
la	**receptionist** *(pl inv)*	receptionist
la	**scala**	ladder; staircase
la	**tariffa**	rate, rates
la	**televisione**	television
la	**valigia** *(pl* **-ge***)*	suitcase
la	**vista**	view
le	**toilette**	toilets
un'	**uscita d'emergenza**	fire escape

USEFUL PHRASES

ha un documento di identità? do you have any ID?
a che ora è servita la colazione? what time is breakfast served?
pulire la stanza to clean the room
"non disturbare" "do not disturb"

IMPORTANT WORDS *(masculine)*

un **asciugamano**	towel
il **bagno**	bathroom
il **benvenuto**	welcome
un **interruttore**	switch
il **lavandino**	washbasin
il **prezzo tutto compreso**	all inclusive price
il **reclamo**	complaint
il **rumore**	noise

USEFUL WORDS *(masculine)*

l' **atrio**	foyer
il **capocameriere**	head waiter
il **cuoco** *(pl* **-chi***)*	cook
il **cuscino**	pillow
il **rubinetto**	tap
il **sommellier** *(pl inv)*	wine waiter

USEFUL PHRASES

occupato(a) occupied
libero(a) vacant
pulito(a) clean
sporco(a) dirty
dormire to sleep
svegliarsi to wake up
"con tutte le comodità" "with all facilities"
potrei avere la sveglia domani mattina alle sette, per favore? I'd like a 7 o'clock alarm call tomorrow morning, please
una camera con vista sul mare a room overlooking the sea

IMPORTANT WORDS *(feminine)*

l'	**acqua calda**	hot water
la	**fattura**	bill; invoice
la	**guida turistica** *(pl* **-e -che***)*	guidebook
la	**mancia** *(pl* **-ce***)*	tip
la	**ricevuta**	receipt
la	**saponetta**	bar of soap
la	**vasca** *(pl* **-che***)* **da bagno**	bathtub

USEFUL WORDS *(feminine)*

la	**cassaforte** *(pl* **casseforti***)*	safe
la	**carta igienica**	toilet paper
la	**coperta**	blanket
la	**corrente d'aria**	draught
la	**cuoca** *(pl* **-che***)*	cook

USEFUL PHRASES

una camera con mezza pensione room with half board
ci sediamo fuori? shall we sit outside?
abbiamo cenato all'aperto we were served dinner outside
un albergo a tre stelle a three-star hotel
IVA inclusa inclusive of VAT

house – general

ESSENTIAL WORDS *(masculine)*

un	**(appezzamento di) terreno**	plot of land
un	**appartamento**	flat, apartment
un	**ascensore**	lift
il	**bagno**	bathroom
il	**balcone**	balcony
il	**box** *(pl inv)*	garage
il	**cancello**	gate
il	**condominio**	block of flats
il	**cortile**	(court)yard
un	**edificio**	building
l'	**esterno**	exterior
il	**garage** *(pl inv)*	garage
il	**giardino**	garden
un	**indirizzo**	address
l'	**interno**	interior
il	**mobile**	piece of furniture
i	**mobili**	furniture
il	**numero di telefono**	phone number
il	**paese**	village
il	**parcheggio**	car park; parking space
il	**piano**	floor, storey; piano
il	**pianoterra**	ground floor
il	**pianterreno**	ground floor
il	**quartiere residenziale**	housing estate
il	**riscaldamento (centralizzato)**	(central) heating
il	**seminterrato**	basement
il	**soggiorno**	living room
il	**viale**	avenue
il	**vialetto d'accesso**	drive

USEFUL PHRASES

quando vado a casa when I go home
guardare fuori dalla finestra to look out of the window
a casa mia/tua/nostra at my/your/our house
traslocare to move house
affittare un appartamento to rent a flat

ESSENTIAL WORDS *(feminine)*

la	**camera da letto**	bedroom
la	**cantina**	cellar
la	**casa**	house
la	**chiave**	key
la	**città** *(pl inv)*	town; city
la	**cucina**	kitchen
la	**doccia** *(pl* **-ce***)*	shower
un'	**entrata**	entrance
la	**finestra**	window
la	**parete**	wall
la	**porta**	door
la	**porta d'ingresso**	front door
la	**sala da pranzo**	dining room
le	**scale**	stairs
la	**stanza**	room
la	**via**	street
la	**vista**	view

USEFUL PHRASES

vivo in una casa/un appartamento I live in a house/flat
(al piano) di sopra upstairs
(al piano) di sotto downstairs
al primo piano on the first floor
al pianoterra on the ground floor
in casa at home

house – general

IMPORTANT WORDS *(masculine)*

l'	**affitto**	rent
l'	**alloggio**	accommodation
un	**appartamento ammobiliato**	furnished flat
il	**bilocale**	two-roomed flat
il	**caminetto**	fireplace
il	**camino**	chimney
il	**corridoio**	corridor
il	**gabinetto**	lavatory
il	**lavandino**	washbasin
il	**mobilio**	furniture
il	**monolocale**	studio flat
il	**padrone di casa**	landlord; owner
il	**pianerottolo**	landing
il	**portinaio**	caretaker; concierge
il	**prato**	lawn
il	**proprietario**	owner; landlord
il	**solaio**	attic
il	**tetto**	roof
il	**trasloco** *(pl* **-chi***)*	move
il	**vicino (di casa)**	neighbour

USEFUL WORDS *(masculine)*

un	**attico**	penthouse; loft apartment
il	**campanello**	door bell
l'	**ingresso**	hall; entrance
un	**inquilino**	tenant; lodger
il	**lucernario**	skylight
il	**muro**	wall
il	**parquet** *(pl inv)*	parquet floor
il	**pavimento**	floor
lo	**scaldabagno (elettrico)**	(electric) water heater
lo	**scalino**	step
il	**soffitto**	ceiling
lo	**studio**	study
il	**tubo**	pipe
il	**vetro**	window pane

IMPORTANT WORDS *(feminine)*

la	**casetta di campagna**	cottage
la	**donna delle pulizie**	cleaner
la	**legnaia**	lumber room
la	**manutenzione**	upkeep; maintenance
la	**padrona di casa**	landlady; owner
la	**portinaia**	caretaker; concierge
la	**proprietaria**	owner; landlady
la	**vicina (di casa)**	neighbour

USEFUL WORDS *(feminine)*

un'	**antenna**	aerial
la	**caldaia**	boiler
la	**camera degli ospiti**	spare room
la	**casa popolare**	council flat *or* house
la	**casalinga** *(pl* **-ghe***)*	housewife
la	**decorazione**	decoration
la	**facciata**	front *(of house)*
un'	**imposta**	shutter
un'	**inquilina**	tenant; lodger
la	**mattonella**	tile
la	**persiana**	blind; shutter
la	**piastrella**	tile
la	**portafinestra**	French window
la	**portineria**	caretaker's room
la	**siepe**	hedge
la	**soffitta**	attic
la	**soglia**	doorstep
la	**tegola**	roof tile; slate
la	**tubatura**	pipe
la	**villetta**	detached house
le	**villette a schiera**	terraced houses

USEFUL PHRASES

bussare alla porta to knock at the door
ha suonato il campanello the doorbell's just gone
dall'esterno from the outside
dentro on the inside
fino al tetto up to the ceiling

ESSENTIAL WORDS *(masculine)*

un	**armadietto**	cupboard
un	**armadio**	wardrobe
un	**asciugacapelli** *(pl inv)*	hair dryer
un	**asciugamano**	towel
il	**bidone della spazzatura**	dustbin
il	**cuscino**	pillow; cushion
il	**dentifricio**	toothpaste
il	**forno**	oven
il	**frigo** *(pl inv)*	fridge
il	**frigorifero**	refrigerator
il	**gas**	gas
un	**interruttore**	switch
il	**lavabo**	washbasin
il	**lavandino**	sink
il	**lenzuolo** *(pl f* **lenzuola***)*	sheet
i	**piatti**	dishes
il	**portacenere** *(pl inv)*	ashtray
il	**poster** *(pl inv)*	poster
il	**quadro**	picture
il	**radiatore**	radiator
il	**rubinetto**	tap
il	**sapone**	soap
lo	**specchio**	mirror
lo	**spremiagrumi** *(pl inv)*	juicer
lo	**strofinaccio**	dishtowel, tea towel
il	**tappeto**	carpet, rug
il	**televisore**	television set
il	**tovagliolo**	napkin
il	**vassoio**	tray

USEFUL PHRASES

farsi un bagno to have a bath
farsi una doccia to have a shower
fare le pulizie to do the housework
mi piace cucinare I like cooking

ESSENTIAL WORDS *(feminine)*

l'	**acqua**	water
la	**bilancia** *(pl* **-ce***)*	scales
la	**caffettiera**	coffee maker
la	**casseruola**	saucepan
la	**cassetta delle lettere**	letterbox
la	**coperta**	blanket
la	**doccia** *(pl* **-ce***)*	shower
l'	**elettricità**	electricity
la	**foto** *(pl inv)*	photo
la	**lampada**	lamp
la	**lavatrice**	washing machine
le	**lenzuola**	sheets
la	**luce**	light
la	**pentola**	saucepan
la	**radio** *(pl inv)*	radio
la	**spazzola**	brush
le	**stoviglie**	dishes
la	**sveglia**	alarm clock
la	**televisione**	television
le	**tende**	curtains
la	**vasca** *(pl* **-che***)*	bath

USEFUL PHRASES

guardare la televisione to watch television
alla televisione on television
accendere/spegnere la TV to switch on/off the TV
gettare qualcosa nel bidone della spazzatura to throw sth in the dustbin
lavare i piatti to do the dishes

house – particular

IMPORTANT WORDS *(masculine)*

un	**aspirapolvere** *(pl inv)*	vacuum cleaner
il	**bidé** *(pl inv)*	bidet
il	**bucato**	(clean) washing
il	**calorifero**	radiator
il	**detersivo (in polvere)**	washing powder
il	**detersivo per piatti**	washing-up liquid
il	**fornello**	stove
il	**termosifone**	heater
il	**ventilatore**	electric fan

USEFUL WORDS *(masculine)*

il	**cestino**	wastepaper basket
il	**coperchio**	lid
il	**ferro da stiro**	iron
il	**forno a microonde**	microwave oven
il	**frullatore**	blender
il	**guanciale**	pillow
il	**macinacaffè** *(pl inv)*	coffee grinder
il	**mestolo**	ladle
il	**piumone**	duvet
il	**secchio**	bucket
il	**soprammobile**	ornament
lo	**straccio per la polvere**	duster
lo	**strofinaccio**	dishcloth
il	**tostapane** *(pl inv)*	toaster
il	**vaso**	vase

USEFUL PHRASES

collegare/scollegare un elettrodomestico to plug in/to unplug an appliance
passare l'aspirapolvere to hoover
fare il bucato to do the washing

IMPORTANT WORDS *(feminine)*

la **donna delle pulizie**	cleaner
la **lampadina**	light bulb
la **lavastoviglie** *(pl inv)*	dishwasher
la **padella**	frying pan
la **piastra**	hob
la **pittura**	paint; painting
la **polvere**	dust
la **presa (di corrente)**	socket
la **prolunga** *(pl* **-ghe***)*	extension
la **ricetta**	recipe
la **roba sporca**	(dirty) washing, laundry
la **serratura**	lock
la **spina elettrica**	plug *(electric)*
la **stufa**	heater

USEFUL WORDS *(feminine)*

la **carta da parati**	wallpaper
la **cera**	floor polish
la **coperta elettrica** *(pl* **-e -che***)*	electric blanket
la **gruccia** *(pl* **-ce***)*	coat hanger
le **immondizie**	rubbish
la **maniglia**	door handle
la **moquette** *(pl inv)*	fitted carpet
la **pentola a pressione**	pressure cooker
la **ringhiera**	bannister
la **scala**	ladder; staircase
la **scopa**	broom
la **spugna**	sponge
la **tappezzeria**	upholstery
la **tavola da stiro**	ironing board

USEFUL PHRASES

scopare to sweep (up)
pulire to clean
mettere via le cose to tidy away things
lasciare in giro i giocattoli to leave toys lying about

ESSENTIAL WORDS *(masculine)*

un **acconto**	deposit
un **assegno**	cheque
il **Bancomat®** *(pl inv)*	debit card; cash dispenser, ATM
il **cambio**	exchange
il **centesimo (di euro)**	euro cent
il **codice postale**	postcode
il **contratto telefonico**	phone contract
il **documento (di identificazione)**	ID card
un **errore**	mistake
un **euro** *(pl inv)*	euro
il **fax** *(pl inv)*	fax; fax machine
il **francobollo**	postage stamp
un **impiegato (allo sportello)**	counter clerk
un **indirizzo**	address
il **modulo**	form
il **numero**	number
il **pacchetto**	parcel
il **passaporto**	passport
il **postino**	postman
il **prefisso telefonico**	dialling code
il **prezzo**	price
il **segnale di libero**	dialling tone
un **sms** *(pl inv)*	text message
lo **sportello**	counter
gli **spiccioli**	small change
il **telefono**	telephone
un **ufficio informazioni turistiche**	tourist information office
un **ufficio postale**	post office

USEFUL PHRASES

la banca più vicina the nearest bank

vorrei incassare un assegno/cambiare del denaro I would like to cash a cheque/to change some money

ESSENTIAL WORDS *(feminine)*

la	**banca** *(pl* **-che***)*	bank
la	**banconota**	banknote
la	**biro** *(pl inv)*	Biro®
la	**buca** *(pl* **-che***)* **delle lettere**	postbox
la	**busta**	envelope
la	**carta di credito**	credit card
la	**carta di debito**	debit card
la	**carta d'identità**	ID card
la	**cartolina**	postcard
la	**cassa**	check-out
la	**chiamata**	call
la	**compagnia telefonica** *(pl* **-e -che***)*	phone company
la	**firma**	signature
un'	**impiegata (allo sportello)**	counter clerk
le	**informazioni**	information
la	**lettera**	letter
la	**penna**	pen
la	**posta elettronica**	email *(service)*
la	**postina**	postwoman
la	**risposta**	reply
la	**sterlina**	pound (sterling)

USEFUL PHRASES

una chiamata telefonica a phone call
telefonare a qn to phone sb
alzare la cornetta to lift the receiver
comporre il numero to dial (the number)
pronto – sono il signor Rossi hello, this is Mr Rossi
la linea è occupata the line is engaged
attenda in linea hold the line
ho sbagliato numero I got the wrong number
riattaccare to hang up
vorrei fare una chiamata internazionale I'd like to make an international phone call

IMPORTANT WORDS *(masculine)*

l'	**ADSL**	broadband
il	**cellulare**	mobile (phone)
il	**conto (in banca)**	(bank) account
il	**credito**	credit
il	**domicilio**	home address
il	**gettone**	token
un	**internet caffè** *(pl inv)*	internet café
il	**libretto degli assegni**	cheque book
il	**messaggio di posta elettronica**	email
il	**numero verde**	freephone
un	**operatore telefonico**	operator
il	**pagamento**	payment
il	**portafoglio**	wallet
il	**portamonete** *(pl inv)*	purse
il	**tasso di cambio**	exchange rate
il	**telefono fisso**	landline
il	**traveller's cheque** *(pl inv)*	traveller's cheque
un	**ufficio oggetti smarriti**	lost property office

USEFUL WORDS *(masculine)*

un	**allegato**	attachment
il	**destinatario**	addressee
il	**login** *(pl inv)*	login
il	**mittente**	sender
il	**ricevente**	receiver
un	**ufficio cambio**	bureau de change
il	**vaglia** *(pl inv)* **postale**	postal order

USEFUL PHRASES

sara punto smith chiocciola anywhere punto com sara dot smith at anywhere dot com

www. [voo voo voo punto] www dot

IMPORTANT WORDS *(feminine)*

la **banda larga**	broadband
la **cabina telefonica** *(pl* **-e -che***)*	phone box
la **carta da lettera**	writing paper
la **chiamata telefonica** *(pl* **-e -che***)*	phone call
la **guida telefonica** *(pl* **-e -che***)*	telephone directory
un' **imposta**	tax
la **levata (della posta)**	collection
la **mail** *(pl inv)*	email
un' **operatrice telefonica** *(pl* **-i -che***)*	operator
la **password** *(pl inv)*	password
la **posta**	mail
la **ricarica** *(pl* **-che***)*	top-up (card)
la **ricompensa**	reward
la **scheda telefonica** *(pl* **-e -che***)*	phonecard
la **scheda telefonica prepagata**	prepaid phonecard
la **segreteria telefonica**	voicemail; answering machine
la **spesa extra**	extra charge
le **spese**	expenses
la **tassa**	tax

USEFUL WORDS *(feminine)*

la **carta da regalo**	wrapping paper
la **casella postale**	PO box
la **chiamata internazionale**	international call
la **destinataria**	addressee
la **lettera raccomandata**	registered letter
la **mittente**	sender
la **SIM card** *(pl inv)*	SIM card
la **suoneria**	ringtone

USEFUL PHRASES

ho perso il portafoglio I've lost my wallet
riempire un modulo to fill in a form
in stampatello in block letters
fare una chiamata a carico del ricevente to make a reverse charge call

GENERAL SITUATIONS

qual è il tuo (*or* suo) indirizzo? what is your address?
come si scrive? how do you spell that?
puoi (*or* può) cambiarmi 100 euro? do you have change of 100 euros?
scrivere to write
rispondere to reply
firmare to sign
puoi (*or* può) aiutarmi per favore? can you help me please?
qual è la strada per la stazione? how do I get to the station?
dritto straight on
a destra to (*or* on) the right; **a sinistra** to (*or* on) the left

LETTERS

Caro Carlo Dear Carlo
Cara Anna Dear Anna
Egr. Sig. Dear Sir
Gent. Sig.ra Dear Madam
saluti best wishes
un abbraccio da love from
baci da love from
cordiali saluti kind regards
distinti saluti yours faithfully; yours sincerely
baci e abbracci love and kisses
% PTO

EMAILS

mandare una mail a qn to email sb

MOBILES

mandare un sms a qn to text sb

PRONUNCIATION GUIDE

Pronounced approximately as:

A	ah
B	bee
C	chee
D	dee
E	ay
F	ef-fay
G	djee
H	ak-ka
I	ee
J	ee loonga
K	kap-pa
L	el-lay
M	em-may
N	en-nay
O	oh
P	pee
Q	koo
R	er-ray
S	es-say
T	tee
U	oo
V	vee
W	dop-pya voo
X	eeks
Y	eepsilon
Z	dzay-ta

ESSENTIAL WORDS *(masculine)*

un **avvocato**	lawyer
i **documenti**	papers
il **furto**	burglary; theft
un **incendio**	fire
un **incidente**	accident
il **passaporto**	passport
il **problema**	problem

IMPORTANT WORDS *(masculine)*

un **aggressore**	mugger
il **carabiniere**	policeman
il **colpevole**	culprit
il **commissariato (di polizia)**	police station
il **consolato**	consulate
il **danno** *or* **i danni**	damage
un **esercito**	army
il **governo**	government
il **ladro**	burglar; thief
il **morto**	dead man
il **permesso**	permission
il **poliziotto**	policeman
il **posto di blocco**	checkpoint; roadblock
il **proprietario**	owner
il **rapinatore**	robber
il **rapinatore a mano armata**	armed robber
il **testimone**	witness

USEFUL PHRASES

rubare to steal; to burgle; **rapinare** to rob
mi hanno rubato il portafoglio! someone has stolen my wallet!
illegale illegal; **innocente** innocent
non è colpa mia it's not my fault
aiuto! help!; **al ladro!** stop thief!
al fuoco! fire!; **mani in alto!** hands up!
rapinare una banca to rob a bank
mandare qn in prigione to send sb to prison; **fuggire** to escape
evadere to escape from prison

ESSENTIAL WORDS *(feminine)*

la	**carta d'identità**	ID card
la	**colpa**	fault
l'	**identità** *(pl inv)*	identity
la	**polizia**	police
la	**poliziotta**	policewoman
la	**verità** *(pl inv)*	truth

IMPORTANT WORDS *(feminine)*

un'	**aggressione**	mugging
la	**banda**	gang
la	**borsetta**	handbag
la	**colpevole**	culprit
la	**denuncia** *(pl* **-ce***)*	report
l'	**imposta sul redito**	income tax
la	**ladra**	thief; burglar
la	**manifestazione**	demonstration
la	**morta**	dead woman
la	**morte**	death
la	**multa**	fine
la	**pena di morte**	death penalty
la	**polizza di assicurazione**	insurance policy
la	**proprietaria**	owner
la	**rapina**	hold-up, robbery
la	**rapinatrice**	robber
la	**ricompensa**	reward
la	**spia**	spy
le	**tasse**	taxes
la	**testimone**	witness

USEFUL PHRASES

una rapina a mano armata a hold-up
rapire un bambino to abduct a child
un gruppo di teppisti a bunch of hooligans
in prigione in prison
picchiarsi to fight; **arrestare** to arrest; **accusare** to charge
essere in custodia cautelare to be remanded in custody
accusare qn di qc to accuse sb of sth; to charge sb with sth

USEFUL WORDS *(masculine)*

un **arresto**	arrest
un **assassinio**	murder
il **bottino**	loot
il **cadavere**	corpse
il **carcere**	prison
un **clandestino**	illegal immigrant; stowaway
il **criminale**	criminal
il **delitto**	crime
il **detective** *(pl inv)* **privato**	private detective
il **detenuto**	prisoner
il **dirottamento aereo**	hijacking
il **dirottatore**	hijacker
il **drogato**	drug addict
il **gangster** *(pl inv)*	gangster
il **giudice**	judge
un **imbroglione**	crook
un **immigrato clandestino**	illegal immigrant
un **omicida**	murderer
un **omicidio**	murder
un **ostaggio**	hostage
il **piromane**	arsonist
il **poliziotto**	policeman
il **prigioniero**	prisoner
il **processo**	trial
il **riscatto**	ransom
il **salvataggio**	rescue
lo **sbirro**	cop
il **sequestratore**	kidnapper
il **sequestro**	kidnapping
lo **spacciatore (di droga)**	drugs pusher
lo **sparo**	(gun) shot
il **tentativo**	attempt
un **teppista**	hooligan
il **terrorismo**	terrorism
il **terrorista**	terrorist
il **tossicodipendente**	drug addict
il **trafficante di droga**	drug dealer
il **tribunale**	court

USEFUL WORDS *(feminine)*

l'	**accusa**	the prosecution; charge
un'	**assassina**	murderer
la	**bomba**	bomb
la	**clandestina**	illegal immigrant; stowaway
la	**criminale**	criminal
la	**custodia cautelare**	custody
la	**delinquente**	criminal
la	**detective** *(pl inv)* **privata**	private detective
la	**detenuta**	prisoner
la	**detenzione**	imprisonment
la	**dichiarazione**	statement
la	**difesa**	defence
la	**dirottatrice**	hijacker
la	**droga** *(pl* **-ghe***)*	drug
la	**drogata**	drug addict
la	**fuga** *(pl* **-ghe***)*	escape
la	**giuria**	jury
la	**guardia**	guard; warden
un'	**immigrata clandestina**	illegal immigrant
un'	**inchiesta**	inquiry
un'	**insurrezione**	uprising
la	**legge**	law
la	**lite**	quarrel, argument
la	**multa**	fine
un'	**omicida**	murderer
la	**piromane**	arsonist
la	**pistola**	gun
la	**poliziotta**	policewoman
la	**prigione**	prison
la	**prova**	proof; evidence
la	**retata**	raid
la	**rivolta**	uprising
la	**sequestratrice**	kidnapper
la	**spacciatrice (di droga)**	drugs pusher
la	**teppista**	hooligan
la	**terrorista**	terrorist
la	**tossicodipendente**	drug addict
la	**trafficante di droga**	drug dealer

ESSENTIAL WORDS *(masculine)*

l' **acciaio**	steel
l' **argento**	silver
il **cotone**	cotton
il **cristallo**	crystal
il **cuoio**	leather
il **ferro**	iron
il **gas**	gas
il **gasolio**	diesel
il **legno**	wood
il **metallo**	metal
l' **oro**	gold
il **vetro**	glass

IMPORTANT WORDS *(masculine)*

l' **acciaio inossidabile**	stainless steel
l' **alluminio**	aluminium
il **cartone**	cardboard
il **ferro battuto**	wrought iron
il **mattone**	brick
lo **stato**	condition
il **tessuto**	fabric

USEFUL PHRASES

una sedia di legno a wooden chair
una cassa di plastica a plastic box
un anello d'oro a gold ring
in buone condizioni in good condition
in cattive condizioni in bad condition

ESSENTIAL WORDS *(feminine)*

la **gomma**	rubber
la **lana**	wool
la **pelle**	leather
la **pietra**	stone
la **plastica**	plastic

IMPORTANT WORDS *(feminine)*

la **carta**	paper
la **fibra sintetica** (*pl* **-e -che**)	synthetic fibre
la **seta**	silk
la **stoffa**	fabric

USEFUL PHRASES

una pelliccia a fur coat
una medaglia d'oro a gold medal
un maglione di lana a woollen jumper
arrugginito(a) rusty

USEFUL WORDS *(masculine)*

l' **acrilico**	acrylic
il **bronzo**	bronze
il **carbone**	coal
il **cemento**	concrete
il **filo (di cotone)**	thread
il **filo di ferro**	wire
il **gesso**	plaster
il **lino**	linen
il **liquido**	liquid
il **marmo**	marble
il **materiale**	material
l' **ottone**	brass
il **piombo**	lead
il **pizzo**	lace
il **rame**	copper
il **raso**	satin
lo **stagno**	tin
il **tweed**	tweed
il **velluto**	velvet
il **velluto a coste**	corduroy
il **vimini**	wickerwork

USEFUL WORDS *(feminine)*

l' **argilla**	clay
la **cera**	wax
la **ceramica** *(pl* **-che***)*	ceramics; pottery
la **colla**	glue
la **corda**	string
la **creta**	clay
la **gommapiuma**	foam rubber
la **latta**	tinplate
la **paglia**	straw
la **pelle scamosciata**	suede
la **porcellana**	china
la **tela**	canvas

ESSENTIAL WORDS *(masculine)*

il	**direttore d'orchestra**	conductor
il	**gruppo**	band
il	**musicista**	musician
il	**pianoforte**	piano
lo	**strumento musicale**	musical instrument
il	**violino**	violin

USEFUL WORDS *(masculine)*

un	**accordo**	chord
un	**archetto**	bow
un	**astuccio**	case
il	**basso**	bass guitar
il	**clarinetto**	clarinet
il	**contrabbasso**	double bass
il	**fagotto**	bassoon
il	**flauto**	flute
il	**flauto dolce**	recorder
un	**impianto di amplificazione**	PA system
il	**jazz**	jazz
il	**leggio** *(pl* **-gii***)*	music stand
il	**microfono**	microphone
il	**minidisco** *(pl* **-chi***)*	minidisc
il	**mixer** *(pl inv)*	mixing deck
un	**oboe**	oboe
un	**organo**	organ
gli	**ottoni**	brass
i	**piatti**	cymbals
il	**sassofono**	saxophone
il	**solista**	soloist
lo	**studio di registrazione**	recording studio
gli	**strumenti a corda**	string instruments
gli	**strumenti a fiato**	wind instruments
gli	**strumenti a percussione**	percussion instruments
il	**tamburello**	tambourine
il	**tamburo**	drum
il	**tasto (del piano)**	(piano) key
il	**trombone**	trombone
il	**violoncello**	cello

ESSENTIAL WORDS *(feminine)*

la	**batteria**	drums, drum kit
la	**chitarra**	guitar
la	**direttrice d'orchestra**	conductor
la	**musica**	music
la	**musicista**	musician
un'	**orchestra**	orchestra

USEFUL WORDS *(feminine)*

un'	**armonica** *(pl* **-che***)*	harmonica
un'	**arpa**	harp
la	**bacchetta**	conductor's baton
la	**banda**	brass band
la	**composizione**	composition
la	**corda**	string
la	**cornamusa**	bagpipes
la	**custodia**	case
la	**grancassa**	bass drum
la	**fisarmonica** *(pl* **-che***)*	accordion
la	**nota**	note
la	**registrazione digitale**	digital recording
la	**solista**	soloist
la	**tromba**	trumpet; bugle
la	**viola**	viola

USEFUL PHRASES

suonare un pezzo to play a piece
suonare forte/piano to play loudly/softly
essere intonato(a)/stonato(a) to sing in tune/out of tune
suonare il piano/la chitarra to play the piano/the guitar
suonare la batteria to play drums
Paolo alla batteria Paolo on drums
esercitarsi al pianoforte to practise the piano
suoni in un gruppo? do you play in a band?
una nota falsa a wrong note

CARDINAL NUMBERS

zero	**0**	zero
uno *(m)*, una *(f)*	**1**	one
due	**2**	two
tre	**3**	three
quattro	**4**	four
cinque	**5**	five
sei	**6**	six
sette	**7**	seven
otto	**8**	eight
nove	**9**	nine
dieci	**10**	ten
undici	**11**	eleven
dodici	**12**	twelve
tredici	**13**	thirteen
quattordici	**14**	fourteen
quindici	**15**	fifteen
sedici	**16**	sixteen
diciassette	**17**	seventeen
diciotto	**18**	eighteen
diciannove	**19**	nineteen
venti	**20**	twenty
ventuno	**21**	twenty-one
ventidue	**22**	twenty-two
ventitré	**23**	twenty-three
trenta	**30**	thirty
trentuno	**31**	thirty-one
trentadue	**32**	thirty-two
quaranta	**40**	forty
cinquanta	**50**	fifty
sessanta	**60**	sixty
settanta	**70**	seventy
ottanta	**80**	eighty
novanta	**90**	ninety
cento	**100**	one hundred

CARDINAL NUMBERS *(continued)*

centouno	**101**	a hundred and one
centodue	**102**	a hundred and two
centodieci	**110**	a hundred and ten
centottantadue	**182**	a hundred and eighty-two
duecento	**200**	two hundred
duecentouno	**201**	two hundred and one
duecentodue	**202**	two hundred and two
trecento	**300**	three hundred
quattrocento	**400**	four hundred
cinquecento	**500**	five hundred
seicento	**600**	six hundred
settecento	**700**	seven hundred
ottocento	**800**	eight hundred
novecento	**900**	nine hundred
mille	**1000**	one thousand
milleuno(a)	**1001**	a thousand and one
milledue	**1002**	a thousand and two
duemila	**2000**	two thousand
duemilanove	**2009**	two thousand and nine
diecimila	**10000**	ten thousand
centomila	**100000**	one hundred thousand
un milione	**1000000**	one million
due milioni	**2000000**	two million

USEFUL PHRASES

mille euro a thousand euros; **duemila euro** two thousand euros
un milione di dollari one million dollars
tre virgola due (3,2) three point two (3.2)

ORDINAL NUMBERS

primo(a)	**1º, 1ª**	first
secondo(a)	**2º, 2ª**	second
terzo(a)	**3º, 3ª**	third
quarto(a)	**4º, 4ª**	fourth
quinto(a)	**5º, 5ª**	fifth
sesto(a)	**6º, 6ª**	sixth
settimo(a)	**7º, 7ª**	seventh
ottavo(a)	**8º, 8ª**	eighth
nono(a)	**9º, 9ª**	ninth
decimo(a)	**10º, 10ª**	tenth
undicesimo(a)	**11º, 11ª**	eleventh
dodicesimo(a)	**12º, 12ª**	twelfth
tredicesimo(a)	**13º, 13ª**	thirteenth
quattordicesimo(a)	**14º, 14ª**	fourteenth
quindicesimo(a)	**15º, 15ª**	fifteenth
sedicesimo(a)	**16º, 16ª**	sixteenth
diciassettesimo(a)	**17º, 17ª**	seventeenth
diciottesimo(a)	**18º, 18ª**	eighteenth
diciannovesimo(a)	**19º, 19ª**	nineteenth
ventesimo(a)	**20º, 20ª**	twentieth
millesimo(a)	**1000º, 1000ª**	thousandth
duemillesimo(a)	**2000º, 2000ª**	two thousandth

FRACTIONS

(un) mezzo/(una) mezza	$\frac{1}{2}$	a half
uno(a) e mezzo(a)	$1\frac{1}{2}$	one and a half
due e mezzo(a)	$2\frac{1}{2}$	two and a half
un terzo	$\frac{1}{3}$	a third
due terzi	$\frac{2}{3}$	two thirds
un quarto	$\frac{1}{4}$	a quarter
tre quarti	$\frac{3}{4}$	three quarters
un sesto	$\frac{1}{6}$	a sixth
tre e cinque sesti	$3\frac{5}{6}$	three and five sixths
un settimo	$\frac{1}{7}$	a seventh
un ottavo	$\frac{1}{8}$	an eighth
un nono	$\frac{1}{9}$	a ninth
un decimo	$\frac{1}{10}$	a tenth
un undicesimo	$\frac{1}{11}$	an eleventh
un dodicesimo	$\frac{1}{12}$	a twelfth
sette dodicesimi	$\frac{7}{12}$	seven twelfths
un centesimo	$\frac{1}{100}$	a hundredth
un millesimo	$\frac{1}{1000}$	a thousandth

USEFUL PHRASES
un barattolo di a jar of; a tin *or* can of
un barile di a barrel of
un bicchiere di a glass of
un boccone di a mouthful of
una bottiglia di a bottle of
una cassa di a box of
centinia di hundreds of
un centinaio di (about) a hundred
un chilo di a kilo of
una cucchiaiata di a spoonful of
una decina di persone about ten people
diversi(e) several
a diversi chilometri da a few kilometres from
una dozzina di (about) a dozen
entrambi both of them
un etto di a hundred grams of
una fetta di pane a slice of bread
una fetta di prosciutto a slice of ham
una (gran) quantità di lots of
un gregge di a flock of
un gruppo di a group of
un litro di a litre of
la maggior parte di, gran parte di most (of)
una mandria di a herd of

USEFUL PHRASES

un metro di a metre of
mezza dozzina half a dozen
mezzo(a) half (of)
mezzo litro di half a litre of
migliaia di thousands of
molti(e) many; a lot of
molto(a) a lot (of); much
un mucchio di a pile of; loads of
un pacchetto di a packet of
un paio di a pair of
un pezzo di carta a piece of paper
un pezzo di pane a piece of bread
un piatto di a plate of
a pochi metri da a few metres from
un poco di a little; some
una porzione di a portion of
un pugno di a handful of
un quarto di a quarter of
tre quarti di three quarters of
una scatola di a tin *or* can of
una scodella di a bowl of
una tazza di a cup of
tutti(e) e due both of them
una zolletta di zucchero a lump of sugar

ESSENTIAL WORDS *(masculine)*

un **anello**	ring
il **braccialetto**	bracelet
il **deodorante**	deodorant
il **gioiello**	jewel
un **orologio**	watch
il **pettine**	comb
il **profumo**	perfume
il **rasoio**	razor
il **rasoio elettrico**	electric shaver
lo **shampoo** *(pl inv)*	shampoo
lo **spazzolino da denti**	toothbrush
lo **specchio**	mirror
il **trucco**	make-up

USEFUL WORDS *(masculine)*

l' **acetone**	nail varnish remover
un **asciugacapelli** *(pl inv)*	hairdryer
il **bigodino**	roller
il **ciondolo**	pendant
il **dentifricio**	toothpaste
il **diamante**	diamond
il **dopobarba** *(pl inv)*	aftershave
gli **effetti personali**	personal effects
il **fard** *(pl inv)*	(powder) compact
il **fazzoletto di carta**	tissue
il **fondotinta** *(pl inv)*	foundation
il **gemello**	cufflink
il **maquillage** *(pl inv)*	make-up
il **mascara** *(pl inv)*	mascara
il **nécessaire da toilette** *(pl inv)*	toilet bag
un **ombretto**	eye shadow
un **orecchino**	earring
il **pennello da barba**	shaving brush
il **portachiavi** *(pl inv)*	key-ring; key holder
il **rossetto**	lipstick
lo **smalto per unghie**	nail varnish

ESSENTIAL WORDS *(feminine)*

l'	**acqua di colonia**	eau de cologne
la	**catenina**	chain
la	**crema per il viso**	face cream
la	**spazzola**	brush

USEFUL WORDS *(feminine)*

un'	**acconciatura**	hairstyle
la	**carta igienica**	toilet paper
la	**cipria**	face powder
la	**collana**	necklace
la	**crema da barba**	shaving cream
la	**fede (nuziale)**	wedding ring
la	**manicure** *(pl inv)*	manicure
la	**perla**	pearl
la	**pettinatura**	hairstyle
la	**schiuma da barba**	shaving foam
la	**spilla**	brooch
la	**spugna**	sponge

USEFUL PHRASES

truccarsi to put on one's make-up
struccarsi to take off one's make-up
farsi un'acconciatura to do one's hair
pettinarsi to comb one's hair
spazzolarsi i capelli to brush one's hair
radersi to shave
lavarsi i denti to clean *or* brush one's teeth

plants and gardens

ESSENTIAL WORDS *(masculine)*

un	**albero**	tree
il	**fiore**	flower
il	**giardinaggio**	gardening
il	**giardiniere**	gardener
il	**giardino**	garden
gl	**ortaggi**	vegetables
il	**prato**	lawn
il	**ramo**	branch
il	**sole**	sun
il	**terreno**	land; soil; ground

IMPORTANT WORDS *(masculine)*

il	**cancello**	gate
il	**cespuglio**	bush
il	**mazzo di fiori**	bunch of flowers
il	**recinto**	fence
il	**vialetto**	path; drive

USEFUL PHRASES

piantare to plant
togliere le erbacce to weed
regalare a qn un mazzo di fiori to give sb a bunch of flowers
tagliare l'erba to mow the lawn
"non calpestare" "keep off the grass"
a mio padre piace fare giardinaggio my father likes gardening

ESSENTIAL WORDS *(feminine)*

un'	**aiola**	flower bed
l'	**erba**	grass
la	**foglia**	leaf
la	**pianta**	plant
la	**pioggia** *(pl* **-ge***)*	rain
la	**rosa**	rose
la	**terra**	soil; ground

IMPORTANT WORDS *(feminine)*

un'	**ape**	bee
la	**coltivazione**	cultivation
le	**erbacce**	weeds
l'	**ombra**	shade; shadow
la	**panchina**	bench
la	**radice**	root
la	**vespa**	wasp

USEFUL PHRASES

i fiori stanno crescendo the flowers are growing
per terra on the ground
bagnare i fiori to water the flowers
raccogliere fiori to pick flowers
andare all'ombra to go into the shade
rimanere all'ombra to remain in the shade
all'ombra di un albero in the shade of a tree

USEFUL WORDS *(masculine)*

l'	**autunno**	autumn
un	**annaffiatoio**	watering can
un	**attrezzo**	tool
il	**bocciolo**	bud
il	**bucaneve** *(pl inv)*	snowdrop
il	**caprifoglio**	honeysuckle
il	**ciclamino**	cyclamen
il	**crisantemo**	chrysanthemum
il	**croco** *(pl* **-chi***)*	crocus
il	**dente di leone**	dandelion
il	**fogliame**	leaves
il	**garofano**	carnation
il	**geranio**	geranium
il	**giacinto**	hyacinth
il	**giglio**	lily
il	**girasole**	sunflower
l'	**inverno**	winter
il	**lillà** *(pl inv)*	lilac
il	**mughetto**	lily of the valley
il	**narciso**	daffodil
un	**oleandro**	oleander
un	**orto**	vegetable garden
il	**papavero**	poppy
il	**raccolto**	crop
il	**ranuncolo**	buttercup
il	**rastrello**	rake
il	**roseto**	rose bush
il	**seme**	seed
lo	**stagno**	pond
lo	**stelo**	stalk
il	**suolo**	ground; soil
il	**tagliaerba** *(pl inv)*	lawnmower
il	**tagliasiepe** *(pl inv)*	hedgecutter
il	**tronco** *(pl* **-chi***)*	trunk *(of tree)*
il	**tubo per annaffiare**	(garden) hose
il	**tulipano**	tulip
il	**verme**	worm

USEFUL WORDS *(feminine)*

l'	**azalea**	azalea
l'	**estate**	summer
la	**bacca** *(pl* **-che***)*	berry
la	**begonia**	begonia
la	**campanula**	campanula, bellflower
la	**carriola**	wheelbarrow
un'	**edera**	ivy
la	**farfalla**	butterfly
la	**margherita**	daisy
un'	**orchidea**	orchid
un'	**ortensia**	hydrangea
la	**peonia**	peony
la	**primavera**	spring
la	**primula**	primrose
la	**rugiada**	dew
la	**serra**	greenhouse
la	**siepe**	hedge
la	**spina**	thorn
la	**stella di Natale**	poinsettia
la	**viola pansée**	pansy
la	**violetta**	violet

seaside and boats

ESSENTIAL WORDS *(masculine)*

un	**asciugamano**	towel
il	**bagnante**	swimmer
il	**battello**	passenger boat
il	**bikini** *(pl inv)*	bikini
il	**catamarano**	catamaran
il	**costume da bagno**	swimming trunks; swimsuit
il	**mare**	sea
il	**molo**	quay
il	**nuoto**	swimming
gli	**occhiali da sole**	sunglasses
il	**pescatore**	fisherman
il	**porto**	port, harbour
il	**remo**	oar

IMPORTANT WORDS *(masculine)*

il	**castello di sabbia**	sandcastle
il	**fondo**	bottom
il	**granchio**	crab
il	**lettino**	sun lounger
il	**mal di mare**	seasickness
il	**materassino gonfiabile**	airbed, lilo®
l'	**orizzonte**	horizon
il	**turista**	tourist; holiday-maker
il	**windsurf** *(pl inv)*	surfboard; windsurfing

USEFUL PHRASES

in spiaggia at *or* on the beach
al mare at the seaside; at *or* on the beach
all'orizzonte on the horizon
ha il mal di mare he/she is seasick
nuotare to swim; **affogare** to drown
vado a fare una nuotata I'm going for a swim
tuffarsi in acqua to dive into the water
galleggiare to float

ESSENTIAL WORDS *(feminine)*

l'	**abbronzatura**	suntan
l'	**acqua**	water
la	**bagnante**	swimmer
la	**barca** *(pl* **-che***)*	boat
la	**costa**	coast
un'	**isola**	island
la	**nave**	ship
la	**pietra**	stone
la	**sabbia**	sand
la	**scottatura solare**	sunburn
la	**spiaggia** *(pl* **-ge***)*	beach

IMPORTANT WORDS *(feminine)*

la	**brandina**	sun lounger
la	**crema solare**	suncream
la	**sedia a sdraio**	deckchair
la	**tavola da windsurf**	surfboard
la	**traversata**	crossing
la	**turista**	tourist; holiday-maker

USEFUL PHRASES

in fondo al mare at the bottom of the sea
fare la traversata in barca to cross by boat
abbronzarsi to get a tan
essere nero(a) to be tanned
sa nuotare he/she can swim

USEFUL WORDS *(masculine)*

un	**acquascooter** *(pl inv)*	jet ski
l'	**albero**	mast
un	**aliscafo**	hydrofoil
il	**bagnino**	lifeguard
il	**binocolo**	binoculars
il	**cannocchiale**	telescope
il	**cargo** *(pl inv)*	cargo
il	**ciottolo**	pebble
l'	**equipaggio**	crew
un	**estuario**	estuary
il	**faro**	lighthouse
il	**gabbiano**	seagull
il	**marinaio**	sailor
il	**motoscafo**	speedboat
il	**naufragio**	shipwreck
un	**oceano**	ocean
un	**ombrellone**	beach umbrella
un	**parasole** *(pl inv)*	parasol
il	**pedalò** *(pl inv)*	pedalo
il	**ponte**	bridge
il	**pontile**	pier, jetty
il	**promontorio**	headland
il	**salvagente** *(pl inv)*	lifebelt
il	**secchiello**	bucket
il	**timone**	rudder
il	**traghetto**	ferry

USEFUL WORDS *(feminine)*

le	**alghe**	seaweed
un'	**ancora**	anchor
l'	**aria di mare**	sea air
la	**bagnina**	lifeguard
la	**baia**	bay
la	**balneazione**	bathing
la	**bandiera**	flag
la	**barca** *(pl* **-che)** **da diporto**	pleasure craft
la	**boa**	buoy
la	**brezza di mare**	sea breeze
la	**conchiglia**	shell
la	**corrente**	current
la	**crociera**	cruise
la	**duna di sabbia**	sand dune
la	**foce**	mouth *(of river)*
un'	**insolazione**	sunstroke
la	**marea**	tide
la	**marina**	navy; marina
la	**marinaia**	sailor
un'	**onda**	wave
la	**paletta**	spade
la	**passerella**	gangway
la	**riva**	shore
la	**roccia** *(pl* **-ce)**	rock
la	**schiuma**	foam
la	**scogliera**	cliff
la	**vela**	sail; sailing
la	**zattera**	raft

USEFUL PHRASES

mi sono preso un'insolazione I had sunstroke
con l'alta/la bassa marea at low/high tide
fare vela to go sailing

ESSENTIAL WORDS *(masculine)*

un	**assegno**	cheque
il	**Bancomat®** *(pl inv)*	debit card; cash machine, ATM
il	**centesimo**	cent
il	**centro commerciale**	shopping centre
il	**cliente**	customer
il	**codice a barre**	barcode
il	**commesso**	shop assistant, sales assistant
il	**denaro**	money
un	**euro** *(pl inv)*	euro
il	**fioraio**	flower shop; florist
il	**fruttivendolo**	greengrocer's
i	**grandi magazzini**	department store
un	**ipermercato**	super store
il	**libretto degli assegni**	cheque book
il	**mercato**	market
il	**negozio**	shop
il	**prezzo**	price
il	**regalo**	present, gift
il	**reparto**	department
il	**resto**	change
il	**ribasso**	reduction
i	**saldi**	sales
lo	**sconto**	discount
i	**soldi**	money
il	**supermercato**	supermarket
il	**tabaccaio**	tobacconist's; tobacconist
il	**venditore**	salesman

USEFUL PHRASES

comprare/vendere to buy/to sell
quanto costa? how much does it cost?
a quanto ammonta? how much does it come to?
l'ho pagato 20 euro I paid 20 euros for it
in macelleria/panetteria at the butcher's/bakery

ESSENTIAL WORDS *(feminine)*

un'	**agenzia di viaggio**	travel agent's
l'	**alimentazione**	food
la	**banconota**	banknote
la	**carta di credito del negozio**	store card
la	**carta di credito**	credit card
la	**carta di debito**	debit card
la	**carta fedeltà**	loyalty card
la	**cassa**	checkout; cash desk
la	**cassa automatica**	self-service checkout
la	**cliente**	customer
la	**commessa**	shop assistant, sales assistant
la	**farmacia**	chemist's
la	**lista**	list
la	**macelleria**	butcher's
la	**panetteria**	bakery
la	**pasticceria**	cake shop
la	**pescheria**	fishmonger's
la	**posta**	post office
la	**profumeria**	perfume shop
la	**salumeria**	delicatessen
la	**tabaccheria**	tobacconist's
la	**taglia**	size
la	**venditrice**	saleswoman

shopping

IMPORTANT WORDS *(masculine)*

un	**articolo**	article
il	**banco** *(pl* **-chi***)*	counter
il	**calzolaio**	cobbler
il	**commerciante**	shopkeeper
il	**commercio**	trade
il	**commercio equo e solidale**	fair trade
il	**direttore**	manager
il	**giornalaio**	newsagent
il	**macellaio**	butcher; butcher's
il	**mercatino**	street market
il	**mercatino delle pulci**	flea market
il	**negozio di generi alimentari**	grocer's
il	**negozio di scarpe**	shoe shop
il	**numero di scarpe**	shoe size
il	**panettiere**	baker
il	**parrucchiere**	hairdresser; hairdresser's
il	**pasticciere**	confectioner
il	**pescivendolo**	fishmonger
il	**portafoglio**	wallet
il	**portamonete** *(pl inv)*	purse
il	**reclamo**	complaint
lo	**scontrino**	receipt

USEFUL PHRASES

sto dando un'occhiata I'm just looking
è troppo caro it's too expensive
qualcosa di più economico something cheaper
è a buon prezzo it's cheap
"pagare alla cassa" "pay at the cash desk"
vuole che le faccia un pacchetto regalo? would you like it gift-wrapped?
ci dev'essere un errore there must be some mistake

IMPORTANT WORDS *(feminine)*

la	**biblioteca** *(pl* **-che***)*	library
la	**borsetta**	handbag
la	**calcolatrice**	calculator
la	**commerciante**	shopkeeper
la	**direttrice**	manager
un'	**enoteca** *(pl* **-che***)*	wine shop
la	**fruttivendola**	fruit shop; greengrocer's
la	**giornalaia**	newsagent
la	**libreria**	bookshop
la	**macellaia**	butcher
la	**marca** *(pl* **-che***)*	brand
la	**panettiera**	baker
la	**parrucchiera**	hairdresser
la	**pasticcera**	confectioner
la	**pescivendola**	fishmonger
la	**promozione**	special offer
la	**pulitura (a secco)**	dry-cleaner's
la	**ricevuta**	receipt
la	**scala mobile**	escalator
la	**tintoria**	dry-cleaner's
la	**vetrina**	display case; shop window

USEFUL PHRASES

qualcos'altro? anything else?
s.r.l. (= società a responsabilità limitata) limited liability company
S.p.A. (= società per azioni) joint-stock company
"in vendita qui" "on sale here"
una macchina usata a used car
in offerta on special offer
il caffè del commercio equo e solidale fair-trade coffee

USEFUL WORDS *(masculine)*

l'	**abbigliamento**	clothes
gli	**acquisti**	shopping
un	**affare**	deal
un	**agente immobiliare**	estate agent
i	**beni**	goods
il	**colore**	colour
il	**gerente**	manager
il	**gioielliere**	jeweller's
il	**libraio**	bookseller
il	**negozio di dolciumi**	sweetshop
un	**orologiaio**	watchmaker; clockmaker
un	**ottico**	optician
i	**prodotti**	produce; products
il	**prodotto**	product
lo	**sconto**	discount
il	**videonoleggio**	video shop

USEFUL PHRASES

andare a fare un giro per vetrine to go window shopping
orario di apertura opening hours
pagare in contanti to pay cash
pagare con un assegno to pay by cheque
pagare con la carta di credito to pay by credit card

USEFUL WORDS *(feminine)*

un'	**agente immobiliare**	estate agent
un'	**agenzia di viaggio**	travel agent's
un'	**agenzia immobiliare**	estate agent's
le	**calzature**	footwear
le	**caramelle**	sweets
la	**cartoleria**	stationery shop
la	**cassa di risparmio**	savings bank
la	**coda**	queue
la	**commissione**	errand; commission
la	**droghiera**	grocer
la	**ferramenta**	ironmonger
la	**fila**	queue
la	**filiale**	branch
la	**gerente**	manager
la	**gioielliera**	jeweller
la	**lavanderia automatica**	launderette
la	**libraia**	bookseller
le	**merci**	goods
un'	**orologeria**	watchmaker's; clockmaker's
un'	**orologiaia**	watchmaker; clockmaker
la	**spesa**	purchase; shopping
la	**taglia del collo**	collar size
la	**vendita**	sale

USEFUL PHRASES

in vetrina in the window
andare a fare acquisti to go shopping
fare la spesa to do the shopping
spendere to spend

ESSENTIAL WORDS *(masculine)*

il **basket**	basketball
il **biliardo**	billiards
il **calcio**	football; kick
il **campionato**	championship
il **campione**	champion
il **campo**	field; pitch; course; court
il **campo da golf**	golf course
il **campo da tennis**	tennis court
il **campo di calcio**	football pitch
il **campo sportivo**	sports field
il **ciclismo**	cycling
il **cricket**	cricket
il **ginnasta**	gymnast
il **giocatore**	player
il **gioco** *(pl* **-chi***)*	game; play
il **gol** *(pl inv)*	goal
il **golf**	golf
l' **hockey**	hockey
il **nuoto**	swimming
il **pallone**	ball *(large)*; football
il **risultato**	result
il **rugby**	rugby
gli **scacchi**	chess
lo **sci** *(pl inv)*	skiing; ski
lo **sci d'acqua**	water skiing
lo **sport** *(pl inv)*	sport
lo **stadio**	stadium
il **tennis**	tennis
il **windsurf** *(pl inv)*	windsurfing; surfboard

USEFUL PHRASES

giocare a calcio/tennis to play football/tennis
segnare un gol/un punto to score a goal/a point
tenere il punteggio to keep the score
il campione/la campionessa del mondo the world champion
vincere/perdere una partita to win/lose a match
il mio sport preferito my favourite sport

ESSENTIAL WORDS *(feminine)*

l'	**aerobica**	aerobics
la	**campionessa**	champion
l'	**equitazione**	horse-riding
la	**ginnasta**	gymnast
la	**ginnastica**	gymnastics
la	**giocatrice**	player
la	**marcia**	racewalking
la	**palla**	ball
la	**pallacanestro**	basketball
la	**pallavolo**	volleyball
la	**partita**	match, game
la	**pesca**	fishing
la	**piscina**	swimming pool
la	**pista**	track
la	**rete**	net; goal
la	**squadra**	team
la	**vela**	sailing; sail

USEFUL PHRASES

pareggiare to equalize; to draw
correre to run; **saltare** to jump; **lanciare** to throw
battere qn to beat sb
allenarsi to train
il Liverpool conduce per 2 a 1 Liverpool is leading by 2 goals to 1
un partita a tennis a game of tennis
è socio di un club he belongs to a club
andare a pesca to go fishing
andare in piscina to go to the swimming pool
sai (*or* sa) nuotare? can you swim?
fare sport to do sport
andare in bicicletta to go cycling
fare vela to go sailing
fare jogging/alpinismo to go jogging/climbing
pattini da ghiaccio/a rotelle (ice) skate/roller skates
pattini in linea Rollerblades®
tiro con l'arco/al bersaglio archery/target practice

IMPORTANT WORDS *(masculine)*

un **arbitro**	referee; umpire *(tennis)*
un **incontro**	match
il **punteggio**	score
il **torneo**	tournament

USEFUL WORDS *(masculine)*

un **allenatore**	trainer; coach
l' **alpinismo**	mountaineering
un **avversario**	opponent
il **canottaggio**	rowing
il **cronometro**	stopwatch
il **giavellotto**	javelin
i **Giochi Olimpici**	Olympic Games
l' **intervallo**	half-time
l' **ippodromo**	race course
il **jogging**	jogging
il **parapendio**	paragliding
il **pattinaggio su ghiaccio**	(ice) skating
il **pattino**	skate
il **perdente**	loser
il **portiere**	goalkeeper
il **principiante**	beginner
il **pugilato**	boxing
il **punto**	point
il **remo**	oar
il **salto in alto**	high jump
il **salto in lungo**	long jump
lo **spettatore**	spectator
lo **squash**	squash
i **tempi supplementari**	extra time
il **tiro**	shooting
i **tuffi**	diving
il **vincitore**	winner
il **volano**	shuttlecock; badminton

IMPORTANT WORDS *(feminine)*

l' **atletica**	athletics
le **bocce**	pétanque
la **boxe**	boxing
la **Coppa del Mondo**	World Cup
la **corsa**	race
le **corse dei cavalli**	horse-racing
la **difesa**	defence
l' **ippica**	horse-racing
le **Olimpiadi**	Olympic Games
la **pallina**	ball *(small)*
la **pista da sci**	ski slope
la **slitta**	sledge

USEFUL WORDS *(feminine)*

un' **allenatrice**	trainer, coach
un' **avversaria**	opponent
la **canna da pesca**	fishing rod
un' **eliminatoria**	heat
la **finale**	final
la **lotta libera**	wrestling
la **maglietta**	jersey, shirt
la **perdente**	loser
la **pesca**	fishing
la **pista da pattinaggio**	skating rink
la **pista da pattinaggio su ghiaccio**	ice rink
la **principiante**	beginner
la **racchetta da ping pong**	ping pong bat
la **racchetta da sci**	ski pole
la **racchetta da tennis**	tennis racket
le **scarpe da ginnastica**	sports shoes; trainers
le **scarpe da tennis**	tennis shoes
la **scherma**	fencing
la **spettatrice**	spectator
la **stazione sciistica**	ski resort
la **tappa**	stage
la **tribuna**	stand
la **vincitrice**	winner

theatre and cinema

ESSENTIAL WORDS *(masculine)*

un	**attore**	actor
un	**auditorium** *(pl inv)*	auditorium
il	**biglietto**	ticket
il	**botteghino**	box office
il	**cinema** *(pl inv)*	cinema
il	**circo** *(pl* **-chi***)*	circus
il	**clown** *(pl inv)*	clown
il	**comico**	comedian
il	**costume**	costume
il	**film** *(pl inv)*	film
il	**pagliaccio**	clown
il	**posto (a sedere)**	seat
il	**programma**	programme
il	**pubblico**	audience; public
il	**sipario**	curtain
lo	**spettacolo**	show; performance; showing
il	**teatro**	theatre
il	**western** *(pl inv)*	western

IMPORTANT WORDS *(masculine)*

il	**balletto**	ballet
il	**cartellone**	poster; playbill
un	**intervallo**	interval
il	**primo attore**	leading man

USEFUL PHRASES

andare a teatro/al cinema to go to the theatre/to the cinema
prenotare un posto to book a seat
una poltrona in platea a seat in the stalls
il mio attore preferito/la mia attrice preferita my favourite actor/actress
durante l'intervallo during the interval
entrare in scena to come on stage
interpretare la parte di to play the part of

ESSENTIAL WORDS *(feminine)*

l'	**atmosfera**	atmosphere
un'	**attrice**	actress
la	**colonna sonora**	soundtrack
la	**commedia**	play; comedy
la	**galleria**	the circle
la	**musica** *(pl* **-che***)*	music
l'	**opera**	opera
un'	**orchestra**	orchestra
la	**pagliaccia** *(pl* **-ce***)*	clown
la	**pellicola**	film
la	**platea**	stalls
la	**poltrona**	seat
la	**prima galleria**	dress circle
la	**proiezione**	screening *(of film)*
la	**sala**	screen *(of cinema)*
la	**star** *(m+f pl inv)*	film star
la	**tragedia**	tragedy
un'	**uscita**	exit

USEFUL PHRASES

recitare to play
ballare to dance
cantare to sing
girare un film to shoot a film
"versione originale" "original version"
"con sottotitoli" "subtitled"
"tutto esaurito" "sold out"
applaudire to clap
bis! encore!
bravo! bravo!
un film di fantascienza/d'amore a science fiction film/a romance
un film d'avventura/dell'orrore an adventure/horror film

IMPORTANT WORDS *(masculine continued)*

il	**protagonista**	protagonist; star
il	**sottotitolo**	subtitle
il	**titolo**	title
il	**trucco** *(pl* **-chi***)*	make-up; trick

USEFUL WORDS *(masculine)*

gli	**applausi**	applause
il	**cast** *(pl inv)*	cast
il	**commediografo**	playwright
il	**copione**	script
il	**critico**	critic
il	**direttore artistico**	artistic director
il	**direttore di scena**	stage manager
il	**drammaturgo** *(pl* **-ghi***)*	playwright
il	**guardaroba** *(pl inv)*	cloakroom
il	**loggione**	the "gods"
il	**musical** *(pl inv)*	musical
il	**palco** *(pl* **-chi***)*	box
il	**palco(scenico)**	stage
il	**personaggio**	character
il	**produttore**	producer
il	**regista**	director *(cinema)*; producer *(TV)*
il	**ridotto**	foyer
il	**riflettore**	spotlight
il	**ruolo**	part
il	**serial** *(pl inv)*	serial
lo	**scenario**	scenery; set
lo	**sceneggiatore**	scriptwriter
lo	**schermo**	screen
lo	**spettatore**	member of the audience
il	**suggeritore**	prompter

IMPORTANT WORDS *(feminine)*

la **locandina**	poster
un' **imbeccata**	cue; prompt
la **maschera**	usher; usherette
la **prenotazione**	booking
la **prima attrice**	leading lady
la **protagonista**	protagonist; star

USEFUL WORDS *(feminine)*

la **biglietteria**	ticket office
la **buca** *(pl* **-che***)* **dell'orchestra**	orchestra pit
la **commediografa**	playwright
la **critica** *(pl* **-che***)*	review; critics
la **direttrice di scena**	stage manager
la **drammaturga** *(pl* **-ghe***)*	playwright
la **farsa**	farce
le **luci della ribalta**	footlights
la **messa in scena**	production
la **parte**	part
la **piccionaia**	the "gods"
la **prima**	first night, premiere
la **produttrice**	producer
la **produzione**	production
le **prove**	(dress) rehearsal
le **quinte**	wings
la **rappresentazione**	performance
la **recitazione**	acting
la **regista**	director *(cinema)*; producer *(TV)*
la **scena**	scene
la **sceneggiatrice**	scriptwriter
la **sceneggiatura**	script
la **scenografia**	set design
la **serie** *(pl inv)*	series
la **soap** *(pl inv)*	soap (opera)
la **spettatrice**	member of the audience
la **suggeritrice**	prompter
la **trama**	plot
la **videoclip** *(pl inv)*	music video

ESSENTIAL WORDS *(masculine)*

un **anno**	year
il **fine settimana** *(pl inv)*	weekend
il **giorno**	day
un **istante**	moment; instant
il **mattino**	morning
il **mese**	month
il **minuto**	minute
il **momento**	moment
un **orologio**	watch; clock
il **pomeriggio**	afternoon; evening
il **quarto d'ora**	quarter of an hour
il **secolo**	century
il **secondo**	second
il **tempo**	time

USEFUL PHRASES

a mezzogiorno at midday
a mezzanotte at midnight
oggi today
domani tomorrow
dopodomani the day after tomorrow
ieri yesterday
ieri sera last night, yesterday evening
l'altroieri the day before yesterday
due giorni fa 2 days ago
tra due giorni in 2 days
una settimana a week
quindici giorni a fortnight
ogni giorno every day
che giorno è oggi? what day is it?; what's the date?
al momento at the moment
le tre meno un quarto a quarter to 3
le tre e un quarto a quarter past 3
oggigiorno nowadays
il ventunesimo secolo in the 21st century

ESSENTIAL WORDS *(feminine)*

la **giornata**	day
la **mattina**	morning
la **mezzora**	half an hour
la **notte**	night
un' **ora**	hour
la **sera**	night; evening
la **serata**	evening
la **settimana**	week
la **sveglia**	alarm clock

USEFUL PHRASES

l'anno scorso/prossimo last/next year
la prossima settimana next week
entro mezzora in half an hour
una volta once
due/tre volte two/three times
diverse volte several times
tre volte all'anno three times a year
nove volte su dieci nine times out of ten
c'era una volta once upon a time there was
dieci alla volta ten at a time
che ora è? what time is it?
sai (*or* **sa) che ora è?** have you got the time?
sono le sei/le sei meno dieci/le sei e mezza it is 6 o'clock/10 to 6/ half past 6
sono le due in punto it is 2 o'clock exactly
poco fa a while ago
tra un po' in a while
presto early
tardi late
stanotte last night *(past)*; tonight *(to come)*

IMPORTANT WORDS *(masculine)*

il	**futuro**	future; future tense
il	**giorno dopo**	next day
il	**passato**	past; past tense
il	**presente**	present *(time)*; present tense
il	**ritardo**	delay

USEFUL WORDS *(masculine)*

un	**anno bisestile**	leap year
il	**calendario**	calendar
il	**cronometro**	stopwatch
il	**decennio**	decade
il	**Medio Evo**	Middle Ages
un	**orologio a pendolo**	grandfather clock
un	**orologio da polso**	wristwatch
il	**quadrante**	face *(of clock)*
il	**sorgere del sole**	sunrise
il	**tramonto**	sunset

USEFUL PHRASES

due giorni dopo two days later
il giorno prima the day before
ogni secondo giorno every other day
in futuro in the future
un giorno di ferie a day off
un giorno festivo a public holiday
un giorno lavorativo a weekday
in un giorno di pioggia on a rainy day
all'alba at dawn
la mattina/sera seguente the following morning/evening
adesso now

USEFUL WORDS *(feminine)*

l'	**alba**	dawn
un'	**epoca** (*pl* **-che**)	time; era
le	**lancette**	hands *(of clock)*
la	**vigilia**	eve

USEFUL PHRASES

sei (*or* **è) in ritardo** you are late
sei (*or* **è) in anticipo** you are early
quest'orologio va avanti/indietro this watch is fast/slow
arrivare puntuale to arrive on time
quanto tempo? how long?
nel terzo millennio the third millennium
dormire fino a tardi to have a lie-in
da un momento all'altro any minute now
tra una settimana in a week's time
lunedì otto a week on Monday
la notte prima the night before
a quel tempo at that time

tools

ESSENTIAL WORDS *(masculine)*

il	**bricolage**	DIY
il	**fai da te**	DIY
un	**attrezzo**	tool

USEFUL WORDS *(masculine)*

un	**ago** *(pl* **-ghi***)*	needle
il	**badile**	spade
il	**cacciavite** *(pl inv)*	screwdriver
il	**chiodo**	nail
un	**elastico**	rubber band
il	**filo spinato**	(barbed) wire
il	**forcone**	(garden) fork
il	**lucchetto**	padlock
il	**martello**	hammer
il	**martello pneumatico**	pneumatic drill
il	**metro a nastro**	tape measure
il	**nastro adesivo**	sticky tape
il	**pennello**	paintbrush
il	**piccone**	pickaxe
lo	**scalpello**	chisel
lo	**scotch** *(pl inv)*	Sellotape®
il	**secchio**	bucket
il	**trapano**	drill
il	**tuttofare** *(pl inv)*	handyman

USEFUL PHRASES

fare qualche lavoretto to do odd jobs
battere un chiodo con il martello to hammer in a nail
"pittura fresca" "wet paint"
pitturare to paint
mettere la carta da parati to wallpaper

ESSENTIAL WORDS *(feminine)*

la	**chiave**	key
la	**chiave inglese**	spanner
la	**corda**	rope
la	**macchina**	machine
un'	**officina**	workshop

USEFUL WORDS *(feminine)*

la	**batteria**	battery
la	**carta vetrata**	sandpaper
la	**cassetta degli attrezzi**	toolbox
la	**colla**	glue
le	**forbici**	scissors
un'	**impalcatura**	scaffolding
la	**lima**	file
la	**molla**	spring
la	**pala**	shovel
la	**pila**	battery *(in radio etc)*; torch
le	**pinze**	pliers
la	**puntina da disegno**	drawing pin
la	**scala (a libretto)**	(step)ladder
la	**sega** *(pl* **-ghe***)*	saw
la	**serratura**	lock
la	**tavola (di legno)**	plank
la	**tuttofare** *(pl inv)*	handywoman
la	**vernice** *(pl inv)*	varnish
la	**vite**	screw

USEFUL PHRASES

"lavori in corso: vietato l'accesso" "construction site: keep out"
pratico(a) handy
tagliare to cut
riparare to mend
avvitare to screw (in)
svitare to unscrew

ESSENTIAL WORDS *(masculine)*

un	**abitante**	inhabitant
un	**albergo** *(pl* **-ghi***)*	hotel
un	**angolo**	corner
un	**autobus** *(pl inv)*	bus
il	**caffè** *(pl inv)*	café; coffee
il	**centro (della città)**	town centre
il	**cinema** *(pl inv)*	cinema
il	**commissariato di polizia**	police station
il	**comune**	town hall
il	**condominio**	block of flats
i	**dintorni**	surroundings
il	**distributore di benzina**	petrol station
il	**duomo**	cathedral
un	**edificio**	building
il	**giro**	tour
l'	**inquinamento (dell'aria)**	(air) pollution
il	**mercato**	market
il	**municipio**	town hall
il	**museo**	museum; art gallery
il	**negozio**	shop
il	**parcheggio**	car park; parking space
il	**parco** *(pl* **-chi***)*	park
il	**pedone**	pedestrian
il	**poliziotto**	policeman
il	**ponte**	bridge
il	**posteggio dei taxi**	taxi rank
il	**quartiere**	district
il	**quartiere degradato**	slum area
il	**ristorante**	restaurant
il	**sobborgo** *(pl* **-ghi***)*	suburb
il	**taxi** *(pl inv)*	taxi
il	**teatro**	theatre
il	**turista**	tourist
un	**ufficio**	office
un	**ufficio postale**	post office

ESSENTIAL WORDS *(feminine)*

un' **abitante**	inhabitant
un' **automobile**	car
la **banca** *(pl* **-che***)*	bank
la **casa popolare**	council house
la **cattedrale**	cathedral
la **città** *(pl inv)*	town, city
la **corriera**	bus; coach
la **fabbrica** *(pl* **-che***)*	factory
la **fermata dell'autobus**	bus stop
la **lavanderia automatica**	launderette
la **macchina**	car
la **metropolitana**	underground, subway
la **panchina**	bench
la **piazza**	square
la **piscina**	swimming pool
la **polizia**	police
la **poliziotta**	policewoman
la **posta**	post office
la **stazione (ferroviaria)**	(train) station
la **stazione delle corriere**	bus station
la **strada**	road
la **torre**	tower
la **turista**	tourist
la **via**	street
la **vista**	view

USEFUL PHRASES

vado in città I'm going into town
in centro in the town centre
nella piazza in the square
una strada a senso unico a one-way street
"vietato l'accesso" "no entry"
attraversare la strada to cross the road

IMPORTANT WORDS *(masculine)*

un	**abbonamento**	season ticket
un	**agente di polizia**	police officer
il	**cartello**	notice; sign
il	**castello**	castle
il	**centro storico**	old town
il	**distributore di biglietti**	ticket machine
il	**giardino pubblico**	park
il	**giornalaio**	news stand
un	**incrocio**	crossroads
un	**ingorgo** *(pl* **-ghi***)*	traffic jam
un	**internet caffè** *(pl inv)*	internet café
il	**marciapiedi** *(pl inv)*	pavement
il	**monumento**	monument
il	**parchimetro**	parking meter
il	**parco** *(pl* **-chi***)*	park
il	**passante**	passer-by
il	**posto**	place
il	**semaforo**	traffic lights
il	**sindaco**	mayor
il	**supermercato**	supermarket
il	**traffico**	traffic
lo	**zoo** *(pl inv)*	zoo

USEFUL PHRASES

all'angolo della strada at the corner of the street
vivere in periferia to live in the outskirts
camminare to walk
prendere l'autobus/la metropolitana to take the bus/the underground
comprare un biglietto multicorse to buy a multiple-journey ticket
timbrare il biglietto to punch the ticket

IMPORTANT WORDS *(feminine)*

un'	**agente di polizia**	police officer
la	**biblioteca** *(pl* **-che***)*	library
la	**chiesa**	church
la	**circolazione**	traffic
la	**città vecchia**	old town
la	**deviazione**	diversion
un'	**edicola**	newspaper kiosk
la	**moschea**	mosque
la	**passante**	passer-by
la	**pinacoteca**	art gallery
la	**sinagoga** *(pl* **-ghe***)*	synagogue
la	**stazione di servizio**	petrol station
la	**via principale**	main street
la	**zona**	zone; area
la	**zona a traffico limitato**	restricted traffic zone
la	**zona industriale**	industrial estate
la	**zona pedonale**	pedestrian precinct

USEFUL PHRASES

industriale industrial
storico(a)historic
bello(a) pretty
brutto(a) ugly
pulito(a)clean
sporco(a) dirty

USEFUL WORDS *(masculine)*

un	**attraversamento pedonale**	pedestrian crossing
il	**bar** *(pl inv)*	café-bar
il	**bastione**	rampart
il	**caffè** *(pl inv)*	coffee shop, café
il	**carcere**	prison
il	**cartello stradale**	road sign
il	**cimitero**	cemetery
il	**ciottolo**	cobblestone
il	**cittadino**	citizen
il	**consiglio comunale**	town council
il	**dépliant** *(pl inv)*	leaflet
il	**distretto**	district
il	**furgone dei traslochi**	delivery van
il	**grattacielo**	skyscraper
il	**lampione**	street lamp
i	**luoghi d'interesse**	sights, places of interest
il	**manifestino**	leaflet
il	**passeggino**	pushchair
il	**quartiere residenziale**	residential area
il	**sondaggio d'opinione**	opinion poll
il	**vicolo cieco** *(pl* **-i -chi***)*	cul-de-sac, dead end
il	**volantino**	flyer, leaflet

USEFUL WORDS *(feminine)*

la **carrozzina**	pram
la **caserma dei pompieri**	fire station
la **cittadina**	citizen
la **coda**	queue
la **curva**	bend
la **fermata dell'autobus**	bus stop
la **fognatura**	sewer
la **folla**	crowd
la **freccia** *(pl* **-ce***)*	arrow
la **galleria d'arte**	art gallery
un' **isola pedonale**	traffic island
la **periferia**	outskirts
la **pista ciclabile**	cycle path; cycle lane
la **popolazione**	population
la **prigione**	prison
la **processione**	procession
la **sfilata**	parade
la **statua**	statue
la **strada senza uscita**	cul-de-sac, dead end
le **strisce pedonali**	zebra crossing
la **superficie stradale**	road surface

ESSENTIAL WORDS *(masculine)*

un	**armadietto per i bagagli**	left-luggage locker
l'	**arrivo**	arrival
il	**bagaglio**	luggage
il	**bar della stazione**	station buffet
il	**biglietto**	ticket
il	**biglietto di andata e ritorno**	return ticket
il	**biglietto di sola andata**	single ticket
il	**binario**	platform; track
il	**buffet della stazione** *(pl inv)*	station buffet
il	**deposito bagagli**	left-luggage office
il	**doganiere**	customs officer
il	**facchino**	porter
il	**freno**	brake
un	**intercity** *(pl inv)*	intercity train
il	**numero**	number
un	**orario**	timetable
il	**parcheggio dei taxi**	taxi rank
il	**passaporto**	passport
il	**ponte**	bridge
il	**portafoglio**	wallet
il	**posto (a sedere)**	seat
il	**ritardo**	delay
lo	**scompartimento**	compartment
lo	**scontrino**	ticket; receipt
il	**supplemento**	extra charge *(to be paid on intercity)*
il	**taxi** *(pl inv)*	taxi
il	**treno**	train
il	**treno ad alta velocità**	high-speed train
il	**treno regionale**	local stopping train
un	**ufficio oggetti smarriti**	lost property office
il	**vagone**	carriage
il	**viaggiatore**	traveller
il	**viaggio**	journey

ESSENTIAL WORDS *(feminine)*

la **bici** *(pl inv)*	bike
la **bicicletta**	bicycle
la **biglietteria**	ticket office
la **borsa**	bag
la **borsetta**	handbag
la **cartina stradale**	map
la **classe**	class
la **coincidenza**	connection
la **direzione**	direction
la **dogana**	customs
la **doganiera**	customs officer
la **fermata della metropolitana**	underground station
le **informazioni**	information
la **linea**	line
la **metropolitana**	underground, subway
la **partenza**	departure
la **prenotazione**	reservation
la **riduzione**	reduction
la **sala d'aspetto**	waiting room
la **stazione**	station
la **tariffa**	fare
la **valigia** *(pl* **-gie** *or* **-ge***)*	suitcase
la **viaggiatrice**	traveller

USEFUL PHRASES

prenotare un posto to book a seat
pagare un supplemento to pay an extra charge, to pay a surcharge
fare/disfare i bagagli to pack/unpack

trains

IMPORTANT WORDS *(masculine)*

un	**allarme**	alarm
il	**cancello**	barrier
il	**carnet di biglietti** *(pl inv)*	book of tickets
il	**confine**	border
il	**controllore**	ticket collector
il	**guidatore**	driver
il	**vagone letto** *(pl* **-i ~***)*	sleeping car
il	**vagone ristorante** *(pl* **-i ~***)*	dining car

USEFUL WORDS *(masculine)*

un	**abbonamento**	season ticket
il	**bagagliaio**	trunk
il	**capostazione** *(pl* **capistazione***)*	stationmaster
il	**deragliamento**	derailment
il	**fischietto**	whistle
il	**macchinista**	engine-driver
il	**passaggio a livello**	level crossing
il	**tabellone**	noticeboard
il	**treno merci** *(pl* **-i ~***)*	goods train
il	**vagone**	carriage
il	**viaggio**	journey; trip

USEFUL PHRASES

prendere il treno to take the train
perdere il treno to miss the train
convalidare il biglietto to date stamp a ticket
salire in treno to get on the train
scendere dal treno to get off the train
è libero questo posto? is this seat free?
il treno è in ritardo the train is late
"è vietato sporgersi dal finestrino" "do not lean out of the window"

IMPORTANT WORDS *(feminine)*

la **carrozza**	carriage
la **cuccetta**	couchette
la **destinazione**	destination
la **durata**	length (of time)
la **ferrovia**	railway
la **frontiera**	border
la **mancia** *(pl* **-ce***)*	tip
la **scala mobile**	escalator
la **tariffa**	fare
Trenitalia	Italian Railway

USEFUL WORDS *(feminine)*

la **capostazione** *(pl inv)*	stationmaster
un' **etichetta**	label
la **locomotiva**	locomotive
la **macchinista**	engine-driver
le **rotaie**	rails

USEFUL PHRASES

vengo con te alla stazione I'll go to the station with you
ti accompagno alla stazione I'll take you to the station
vengo a prenderti alla stazione I'll come and pick you up at the station
il treno delle dieci diretto a/proveniente da Roma the 10 o'clock train to/ from Rome

ESSENTIAL WORDS *(masculine)*

un **albero**	tree
il **bosco** *(pl* **-chi***)*	wood
il **ramo**	branch

USEFUL WORDS *(masculine)*

un **abete**	fir tree
un **acero**	maple
un **agrifoglio**	holly
un **albero da frutta**	fruit tree
un **albicocco** *(pl* **-chi***)*	apricot tree
un **arancio**	orange tree; orange
un **arbusto**	shrub
il **fico** *(pl* **-chi***)*	fig tree; fig
il **leccio**	ilex, holm oak
il **banano**	banana tree
il **biancospino**	hawthorn
il **bocciolo**	bud
il **bosso**	box tree
il **castagno**	chestnut tree
il **cespuglio**	bush
il **ciliegio**	cherry tree
il **faggio**	beech
il **fogliame**	foliage
il **frassino**	ash
il **limone**	lemon tree; lemon
il **melo**	apple tree
il **noce**	walnut tree
un **olmo**	elm
un **orto**	orchard
il **pero**	pear tree
il **pesco** *(pl* **-chi***)*	peach tree
il **pino**	pine
il **pioppo**	poplar
il **platano**	plane tree
il **rovere**	oak
il **salice piangente**	weeping willow
il **tiglio**	lime tree
il **tronco** *(pl* **-chi***)*	trunk

ESSENTIAL WORDS *(feminine)*

la **foglia**	leaf
la **foresta**	forest
la **foresta pluviale**	rain forest
la **palma**	palm tree

USEFUL WORDS *(feminine)*

la **bacca** *(pl* **-che***)*	berry
la **betulla**	birch
la **corteccia** *(pl* **-ce***)*	bark
la **foresta**	forest
la **gemma**	bud
la **radice**	root
la **vigna**	vineyard

vegetables

ESSENTIAL WORDS *(masculine)*

l'	**aglio**	garlic
il	**cavolfiore**	cauliflower
i	**fagiolini**	French beans
i	**funghi**	mushrooms
gli	**ortaggi**	vegetables
il	**peperone**	pepper
i	**piselli**	peas
il	**pomodoro**	tomato

USEFUL WORDS *(masculine)*

un	**asparago**	asparagus
il	**basilico**	basil
i	**broccoli**	broccoli
il	**carciofo**	artichoke
i	**cavoletti di Bruxelles**	Brussels sprouts
il	**cavolo**	cabbage
i	**ceci**	chickpeas
il	**cetriolo**	cucumber
il	**cipollotto**	spring onion
i	**fagioli**	beans
i	**fagioli bianchi**	haricot beans
i	**(fagioli) borlotti**	kidney beans
i	**legumi**	pulses
il	**mais**	sweetcorn
il	**porro**	leek
il	**prezzemolo**	parsley
il	**ravanello**	radish
il	**sedano**	celery
gli	**spinaci**	spinach

USEFUL PHRASES

coltivare ortaggi to grow vegetables
una pannocchia bollita corn on the cob

ESSENTIAL WORDS *(feminine)*

la **carota**	carrot
la **cipolla**	onion
l' **insalata**	salad
la **patata**	potato
le **verdure**	vegetables

USESFUL WORDS *(feminine)*

la **barbabietola**	beetroot
la **cicoria**	chicory
l' **indivia**	endive
la **lattuga**	lettuce
le **lenticchie**	lentils
la **melanzana**	aubergine
la **rapa**	turnip
la **scarola**	curly endive
la **zucca** *(pl* **-che***)*	pumpkin
la **zucchina**	courgette

USEFUL PHRASES

carote grattugiate grated carrot
biologico(a) organic
vegetariano(a) vegetarian

ESSENTIAL WORDS *(masculine)*

un	**aereo**	plane
un	**aeroplano**	aeroplane
un	**autobus** *(pl inv)*	bus
il	**camion** *(pl inv)*	lorry
il	**camper** *(pl inv)*	camper van
il	**casco** *(pl* **-chi***)*	helmet
il	**ciclomotore**	moped
un	**elicottero**	helicopter
il	**ferry** *(pl inv)*	ferry
il	**furgone**	van
il	**mezzo di trasporto**	means of transport
il	**motorino**	moped
il	**prezzo del biglietto**	fare
lo	**scooter** *(pl inv)*	scooter
il	**taxi** *(pl inv)*	taxi
il	**tir** *(pl inv)*	heavy goods vehicle
il	**traghetto**	ferry
i	**trasporti pubblici**	public transport
il	**treno**	train
il	**veicolo**	vehicle
il	**veliero**	sailing ship

IMPORTANT WORDS *(masculine)*

il	**camion** *(pl inv)* **dei pompieri**	fire engine
il	**carro attrezzi**	breakdown van

USEFUL PHRASES

viaggiare to travel
ha preso un aereo per Palermo he/she flew to Palermo
prendere l'autobus/la metropolitana/il treno to take the bus/the subway/the train
andare in bicicletta to go cycling
ci si può andare in macchina you can go there by car

ESSENTIAL WORDS *(feminine)*

un'	**auto** *(pl inv)*	car
un'	**automobile**	car
la	**barca** *(pl* **-che***)*	boat
la	**barca** *(pl* **-che***)* **a remi**	rowing boat
la	**barca** *(pl* **-che***)* **a vela**	sailing boat
la	**bici** *(pl inv)*	bike
la	**bicicletta**	bicycle
la	**corriera**	coach
la	**distanza**	distance
la	**funicolare**	funicular railway
la	**macchina**	car
la	**metropolitana**	underground, subway
la	**moto** *(pl inv)*	motorbike
la	**motocicletta**	motorcycle, motorbike
la	**parte anteriore**	front
la	**parte posteriore**	back
la	**roulotte** *(pl inv)*	caravan
la	**vespa®**	vespa®

IMPORTANT WORDS *(feminine)*

un'	**ambulanza**	ambulance
un'	**autopompa**	fire engine

USEFUL PHRASES

riparare la macchina a qn to repair sb's car
una macchina a noleggio a hire car
una macchina sportiva a sports car
una macchina da corsa a racing car
la macchina della ditta the company car
"auto usate" "used cars"
partire to start, to move off
to sit in the front/back sedersi davanti/dietro

USEFUL WORDS *(masculine)*

un **aliante**	glider
un **aliscafo**	hydrofoil
un **autoarticolato**	articulated lorry
un **autocarro**	lorry
il **bulldozer** *(pl inv)*	bulldozer
il **camion cisterna** *(pl inv)*	tanker lorry
il **carro**	cart
il **carro armato**	tank
il **disco volante** *(pl* **-chi -i***)*	flying saucer
il **fuoristrada** *(pl inv)*	jeep, off-road vehicle
il **furgone dei traslochi**	delivery van
il **gommone**	rubber dinghy
un **hovercraft** *(pl inv)*	hovercraft
un **idrovolante**	seaplane
il **motore**	engine
il **motoscafo**	speedboat
il **passeggino**	pushchair
il **razzo**	rocket
il **rimorchiatore**	tug
il **rimorchio**	trailer
il **sottomarino**	submarine
il **suv** *(pl inv)*	suv
il **tram** *(pl inv)*	tram
il **trattore**	tractor
un **ufo** *(pl inv)*	UFO *(unidentified flying object)*
lo **yacht** *(pl inv)*	yacht

USEFUL WORDS *(feminine)*

un'	**astronave**	spaceship
una	**barca** *(pl* **-che)** **da diporto**	pleasure boat
la	**canoa**	canoe
la	**carrozzina**	pram
la	**chiatta**	barge
la	**funivia**	cable car
un'	**imbarcazione**	boat
la	**jeep** *(pl inv)*	jeep
la	**lancia** *(pl* **-ce)**	launch
la	**lancia** *(pl* **-ce)** **di salvataggio**	lifeboat
la	**locomotiva**	locomotive
la	**macchina familiare**	estate car
la	**monovolume** *(pl inv)*	people carrier
la	**nave**	ship
la	**nave cisterna** *(pl* **-i ~)**	tanker (ship); water supply ship
la	**navetta**	shuttle bus
la	**petroliera**	oil tanker *(ship)*
la	**portaerei** *(pl inv)*	aircraft carrier
la	**seggiovia**	chairlift
la	**station wagon** *(pl inv)*	estate car

ESSENTIAL WORDS *(masculine)*

l' **autunno**	autumn
il **bollettino meteo**	weather report
il **calore**	heat
il **cielo**	sky
il **clima**	climate
l' **est**	east
il **freddo**	cold
il **grado**	degree
il **ghiaccio**	ice
l' **inverno**	winter
il **meteo** *(pl inv)*	weather report
il **nord**	north
l' **ovest**	west
un **ombrello**	umbrella
il **sole**	sun; sunshine
il **sud**	south
il **tempo**	weather
il **vento**	wind

USEFUL PHRASES

che tempo fa? what's the weather like?
fa caldo/freddo it's hot/cold
è una bella giornata it's a lovely day
è una brutta giornata it's a horrible day
all'aria aperta in the open air
c'è nebbia it's foggy
30° all'ombra 30° in the shade
ascoltare le previsioni del tempo to listen to the weather forecast
piovere to rain
nevicare to snow
c'è il sole it's sunny
c'è vento it's windy
piove it's raining
nevica it's snowing

ESSENTIAL WORDS *(feminine)*

l' **aria**	air
l' **estate**	summer
la **nebbia**	fog
la **neve**	snow
la **nuvola**	cloud
la **pioggia** *(pl* **-ge***)*	rain
le **previsioni del tempo**	(weather) forecast
la **primavera**	spring
la **regione**	region, area
la **stagione**	season
la **temperatura**	temperature

USEFUL PHRASES

brilla il sole the sun is shining
soffia il vento the wind is blowing
si gela it's freezing
gelare to freeze
c'è stata una gelata there's been a frost
sciogliersi to melt
una giornata di sole a sunny day
una giornata di pioggia a rainy day
tempestoso(a) stormy
fresco(a) cool
variable changeable
umido(a)humid
è coperto the sky is overcast

IMPORTANT WORDS *(masculine)*

il **buio**	darkness
il **fumo**	smoke
il **rovescio**	shower

USEFUL WORDS *(masculine)*

un **acquazzone**	downpour
un **arcobaleno**	rainbow
il **barometro**	barometer
il **cambiamento**	change
il **chiaro di luna**	moonlight
il **crepuscolo**	nightfall, dusk
il **cumulo di neve**	snowdrift
il **disgelo**	thaw
il **fiocco** *(pl* **-chi***)* **di neve**	snowflake
il **fulmine**	flash of lightning
il **ghiacciolo**	icicle
il **miglioramento**	improvement
il **parafulmine** *(pl inv)*	lightning conductor
il **raggio di sole**	ray of sunshine
lo **spazzaneve** *(pl inv)*	snowplough
il **temporale**	thunderstorm
il **tramonto**	sunset
il **tuono**	thunder
un **uragano**	hurricane

IMPORTANT WORDS *(feminine)*

la	**burrasca** *(pl* **-che***)*	storm
la	**polvere**	dust
le	**precipitazioni**	rainfall
la	**schiarita**	sunny spell
la	**tempesta**	storm
la	**tormenta**	storm
la	**tromba d'aria**	whirlwind
la	**visibilità**	visibility

USEFUL WORDS *(feminine)*

l'	**alba**	dawn, daybreak
un'	**alluvione**	flood
l'	**atmosfera**	atmosphere
la	**brezza**	breeze
la	**brina**	frost *(on the ground)*
la	**corrente (d'aria)**	draught
la	**foschia**	mist
la	**gelata**	frost
la	**goccia di pioggia**	raindrop
la	**grandine**	hail
un'	**inondazione**	flood
la	**nevicata**	snowfall
un'	**ondata di caldo**	heatwave
l'	**oscurità**	darkness
la	**pozzanghera**	puddle
la	**raffica di vento**	gust of wind
la	**rugiada**	dew
la	**siccità**	drought

youth hostelling

ESSENTIAL WORDS *(masculine)*

il	**bagno**	bathroom
il	**bidone delle immondizie**	dustbin
il	**dormitorio**	dormitory
i	**gabinetti**	lavatories
il	**lenzuolo** *(pl f* **lenzuola***)*	sheet
i	**letti a castello**	bunk bed
il	**letto**	bed
il	**listino dei prezzi**	price list
un	**ospite**	visitor
un	**ostello della gioventù**	youth hostel
il	**pasto**	meal
il	**rifugio**	mountain hostel
i	**servizi**	toilets
il	**silenzio**	silence
il	**soggiorno**	stay; living room
un	**ufficio**	office

IMPORTANT WORDS *(masculine)*

il	**lavandino**	washbasin
il	**regolamento**	rules
il	**sacco** *(pl* **-chi***)* **a pelo**	sleeping bag
lo	**zaino**	rucksack

ESSENTIAL WORDS *(feminine)*

la	**cartina**	map
la	**colazione**	breakfast
la	**cucina**	kitchen; cooking
la	**doccia** *(pl* **-ce***)*	shower
le	**lenzuola**	sheets
la	**notte**	night
un'	**ospite**	visitor
la	**sala giochi**	games room
la	**stanza da pranzo**	dining room
la	**tariffa**	rate
le	**toilette**	toilets
le	**vacanze**	holidays

IMPORTANT WORDS *(feminine)*

la	**biancheria del letto**	bed linen
la	**camminata**	walk
un'	**escursione**	hike; trip
la	**guida**	guidebook; guide
la	**tessera (associativa)**	membership card

USEFUL PHRASES

passare una notte in un ostello to spend a night at the youth hostel
vorrei comprare un sacco a pelo I would like to buy a sleeping bag
non c'è più posto there's no more room

The vocabulary items on pages 204 to 242 have been grouped under parts of speech rather than topics because they can apply in a wide range of circumstances. Use them just as freely as the vocabulary already given.

ARTICLES AND PRONOUNS

What is an article?
An **article** is one of the words *the*, *a* and *an* which is given in front of a noun.

What is a pronoun?
A **pronoun** is a word you use instead of a noun, when you do not need or want to name someone or something directly, for example, *it*, *you*, *none*.

alcuni/alcune some
altrettanto the same
altro/altra: un altro/un'altra another one
altri/altre others
gli altri/le altre other people
ambedue both
che what; which; that
chi who; whoever
chiunque whoever; anyone
ci us; to us; ourselves; each other
ciascuno/ciascuna each
ciò this
cui to whom; of whom; whose
egli he
entrambi both
essi/esse they
esso/a it
gli the; him; to him; it; to it
i the
il the
io I
la the; her; it; you
le the; her; to her; to you; them
lei she;her; you
li them
lo the; him; it
loro they; them; theirs
lui he; him
me me; to me
mi me; to me; myself
mio/mia/miei/mie: il mio/la mia/i miei/le mie mine
ne of it; of them; about it; about them
nessuno/nessuna nobody; no-one; none; anyone
niente nothing
noi we; us
nostro/nostra/nostri/nostre: il nostro/la nostra/i nostri/le nostre ours
nulla nothing; anything
ognuno each; everbody
parecchio/parecchia quite a lot
qualcosa something; anything
qualcuno somebody; someone; anybody; anyone

qual(e) which; what
quanti/quante how many
quanto/quanta how much
quelli/quelle/quegli those ones
quello/quella that one
questi/queste these ones
questo/questa this one
sé himself; herself; itself; themselves; oneself
si oneself; himself; herself; itself; themselves; each other
stesso/stessa: lo stesso/la stessa the same one
gli stessi/le stesse the same ones
suo/sua/suoi/sue: il suo/la sua/ i suoi/le sue his; hers; yours
tanti/tante many; so many
tanto/tanta much, so much
te you; to you
ti you; to you; yourself
troppi/troppe too many
troppo/troppa too much
tu you
tuo/tua/tuoi/tue: il tuo/la tua/ i tuoi/le tue yours
tutti everybody
tutto everything
uno/una a, an; one
ve to you
vi you; to you; yourselves; each other
voi you
vostro/vostra/vostri/vostre: il vostro/la vostra/i vostri/le vostre yours

CONJUNCTIONS

What is a conjunction?
A **conjunction** is a word such as *and*, *but*, *or*, *so*, *if* and *because*, that links two words or phrases of a similar type, or two parts of a sentence, for example, *Diane and I have been friends for years; I left because I was bored*.

a meno che unless
affinché so that
anche too; even
ancora still; even
anzi in fact
anziché rather than; instead of
appena as soon as
benché although
che that; than
come how; as
comunque however
così: così ... che so ... that ...
  così ... come as ... as
dopo after
dunque so; well
e(d) and; but
eppure and yet
finché until; as long as
infatti infact
ma but; however; nevertheless
mentre while
né: né... né... neither... nor...
nonostante even though
o or
  o... o... either... or...
oppure or
perché because; so that
perciò so
però but
per quanto however
pertanto therefore
poiché since
prima di before
purché as long as
pure too; even though
quando when
  da quando since
quindi so
se if; whether
sebbene even though
sia... che... both... and...
siccome since

ADJECTIVES

What is an adjective?
An **adjective** is a 'describing' word that tells you more about a person or thing, such as their appearance, colour, size or other qualities, for example, *pretty*, *blue*, *big*.

abbondante big
abile skilful
abituato(a): abituato a used to
acceso(a) on; burning; lit
accogliente pleasant; welcoming
accurato(a) detailed
acido(a) acid; sour
acuto(a) high; sharp; acute
adatto(a) right (for); suitable
addormentato(a) sleeping; asleep
aderente tight
affascinante very attractive
affaticato(a) tired
affettuoso(a) affectionate
affidabile reliable
affilato(a) sharp
affollato(a) crowded
afoso(a) muggy
aggiornato(a) up-to-date
agitato(a) nervous
allegro(a) cheerful
allucinante awful
alternativo(a) alternative
alto(a) high; tall; loud; deep
altro(a) other
amaro(a) bitter
ambedue both
amichevole friendly
ammalato(a) ill
ammobiliato(a) furnished
ampio(a) spacious; loose
analcolico(a) soft
anonimo(a) anonymous
antipatico(a) unpleasant
antiquato(a) old-fashioned
anziano(a) old
aperto(a) open
appuntito(a) sharp
armato(a) armed
arrabbiato(a) angry
arredato(a) furnished
arrugginito(a) rusty
asciutto(a) dry
aspro(a) sour
assente absent
assetato(a) thirsty
assortito(a) assorted
assurdo(a) ridiculous
astemio(a) teetotal
astratto(a) abstract
astuto(a) cunning
attento(a) careful
attillato(a) tight
attivo(a) active
attrezzato(a) equipped
attuale present; current
avaro(a) mean; stingy
bagnato(a) wet
basso(a) low; short; shallow
beato(a) blessed; lucky
bello(a) lovely; good-looking
benvenuto(a) welcome

biondo(a) blond
bollente boiling
bravo(a) good; clever
breve short
brusco(a) abrupt
brutto(a) ugly; bad
buffo(a) funny
buio(a) dark
buono(a) good
caldo(a) hot; warm
calmo(a) calm
capace able
capriccioso(a) naughty
carino(a) nice; nice-looking
caro(a) dear; expensive
cattivo(a) bad; nasty
celebre famous
certo(a) sure; certain
  certi(e) some
chiaro(a) clear; light; fair
chiuso(a) closed; locked
cieco(a) blind
colpevole guilty
colto(a) well-educated
comodo(a) comfortable
completo(a) complete; full
comprensivo(a) understanding
compreso(a) inclusive
comune common
congelato(a) frozen
conosciuto(a) well-known
contento(a) happy; glad
continuo(a) constant; nonstop
contrario(a) opposite
conveniente cheap
coperto(a) indoor; covered; overcast
corto(a) short
costoso(a) expensive
cotto(a) cooked
crespo(a) frizzy
cretino(a) stupid
croccante crisp; crusty
crudele cruel
crudo(a) raw
dannoso(a) harmful
debole weak
deluso(a) disappointed
denso(a) dense; thick
deprimente depressing
destro(a) right
determinato(a) certain; determined
difettoso(a) faulty
difficile difficult
diffidente suspicious
diffuso(a) common
diligente hard-working
dimagrante slimming
diretto(a) direct; through
diritto(a) straight
disabitato(a) uninhabited
disastroso(a) disastrous
discreto(a) reasonable; discreet
disgustoso(a) disgusting
disinvolto(a) relaxed
disonesto(a) dishonest
disordinato(a) untidy
dispari odd
disperato(a) desperate
dispettoso(a) spiteful
disponibile available
dissetante refreshing; thirst-quenching
distinto(a) distinguished; distinct
distratto(a) absent-minded
disubbidiente disobedient
diversi(e) several

diverso(a) different
divertente funny
dolce sweet
doloroso(a) painful; sad
doppio(a) double
dotato(a) gifted
drammatico(a) dramatic
duro(a) hard
eccellente excellent
eccezionale really good
eccitato(a) excited; aroused
ecologico(a) ecological
economico(a) inexpensive; economic
educato(a) polite
efficace effective
efficiente efficient
egoista selfish
elasticizzato(a) stretch
elementare basic; elementary; primary
elettrico(a) electric
emotivo(a) emotional
emozionante exciting
emozionato(a) moved; emotional
enorme huge
entrambi both
entusiasta enthusiastic; delighted
ereditario(a) hereditary
esatto(a) exact
esaurito(a) sold out; run down
esausto(a) exhausted
esclusivo(a) exclusive
escluso(a) except
esigente demanding
esotico(a) exotic
esplicito(a) explicit
esteriore exterior
esterno(a) outside
estero(a) foreign
estivo(a) summer
estremo(a) extreme
estroverso(a) outgoing
evidente obvious
facile easy
facoltativo(a) optional
falso(a) false; forged; fake
familiare familiar
famoso(a) famous
fantastico(a) great
fastidioso(a) annoying
faticoso(a) tiring
favoloso(a) fabulous
fedele faithful
felice happy
femminile feminine
feriale: giorno feriale week day
fermo(a) still; stopped
festivo: giorno festivo Sunday; holiday
fiero(a) proud
fine thin; fine; refined
finto(a) false; artificial; imitation
fisico(a) physical
fisso(a) fixed; permanent; regular
flessibile flexible
fondo(a) deep
forte strong; loud
fortunato(a) lucky
freddo(a) cold
frequentato(a) popular
frequente frequent
fresco(a) fresh; cool
fritto(a) fried
frizzante sparkling
furbo(a) clever
furibondo(a) furious
gassato(a) fizzy

gelato(a) frozen
gelido(a) icy
geloso(a) jealous
generoso(a) generous
geniale brilliant
gentile nice; kind
ghiacciato(a) frozen
gigante giant
giornaliero(a) daily
giovane young
giusto(a) right
goffo(a) clumsy
gonfio(a) swollen
grande big; great; grown-up
grasso(a) fat
gratuito(a) free
grave serious
grazioso(a) charming
grosso(a) big; large
guasto(a) not working
gustoso(a) tasty
handicappato(a) disabled
ideale ideal
identico(a) identical
idiota stupid
idratante moisturizing
imbarazzante awkward
imbarazzato(a) embarrassed
imbattibile unbeatable
imbottito(a) filled
imbranato(a) awkward; clumsy
immaturo(a) immature
immenso(a) huge
immobile motionless
impacciato(a) awkward
impanato(a) in breadcrumbs
impegnativo(a) demanding
impegnato(a) busy
impermeabile waterproof
impressionante terrible
imprevedibile unpredictable
imprevisto(a) unexpected
improvviso(a) sudden
inaffidabile unreliable
inaspettato(a) unexpected
incantevole lovely
incerto(a) uncertain
incinta pregnant
incluso(a) included
incollato(a) glued
incosciente unconscious; reckless
incustodito(a) unattended
indaffarato(a) busy
indimenticabile unforgettable
indipendente independent
indiretto(a) indirect
indispensabile essential
individuale personal
inesperto(a) inexperienced
infantile childish
infedele unfaithful
infelice unhappy
infinito(a) endless
infortunato(a) injured
infreddolito(a) cold
ingenuo(a) naïve
ingiusto(a) unfair
ingombrante cumbersome
innamorato(a) in love
insicuro(a) insecure
insolito(a) unusual
insopportabile unbearable
integrale wholemeal
internazionale international
interno(a) inside
intero(a) whole
intraprendente enterprising
inutile useless

invadente interfering
invalido(a) disabled
invernale winter
inverso(a) opposite
invidioso(a) jealous
istruito(a) well-educated
largo(a) wide
lavorativo(a) working
leale loyal
leggero(a) light
lento(a) slow
lesso(a) boiled
libero(a) free
limpido(a) clear
liquido(a) liquid
liscio(a) smooth; straight
logico(a) logical
logoro(a) threadbare
lontano(a) distant; far off
loro their
lucido(a) shiny; lucid
luminoso(a) bright; luminous
lunatico(a) temperamental
lungo(a) long
lussuoso(a) luxury
maggiore bigger; older
maggiorenne of age
magico(a) magic
magnetico(a) magnetic
magnifico(a) wonderful
magro(a) thin; low-fat
maiuscolo(a) capital
malato(a) ill, sick
maldestro(a) clumsy
maledetto(a) damn
maleducato(a) rude
malinconico(a) sad
malizioso(a) mischievous
malvagio(a) wicked
mancino(a) left-handed
manuale manual
marcio(a) rotten
maschile male; masculine
maschio(a) male
massimo(a) maximum
materno(a) maternal
matrimoniale matrimonial; double
matto(a) mad
maturo(a) ripe; mature
medesimo(a) same
medico(a) medical
medio(a) average
mensile monthly
meraviglioso(a) wonderful
meridionale southern
mezzo(a) half
migliore better
miliardario(a) billionaire
minimo(a) minimum; minimal
minore less; younger; smaller
minorenne under age
mio(a) my
miope short-sighted
misterioso(a) mysterious
misto(a) mixed
moderno(a) modern
modesto(a) modest
molle soft
molto(a) a lot of; much
  molti(e) many
mondiale world
morbido(a) soft
mortale fatal
morto(a) dead
mosso(a) rough; wavy; blurred
muto(a) dumb; silent
nasale nasal
nascosto(a) hidden

natalizio(a) Christmas
naturale natural; still
nauseante disgusting
necessario(a) necessary
nervoso(a) irritable
nessuno(a) no
netto(a) clear
neutro(a) neutral; neuter
nobile aristocratic
nocivo(a) harmful
noioso(a) boring
nostro(a) our
noto(a) well-known
notturno(a) night
nubile unmarried
nudo(a) naked
numeroso(a) numerous
nuovo(a) new
nutriente nourishing
nuvoloso(a) cloudy
obbediente obedient
obbligatorio(a) compulsory
obiettivo(a) objective
obliquo(a) oblique
occidentale western
occupato(a) occupied
odioso(a) hateful
offeso(a) offended
ogni every
onesto(a) honest
opportuno(a) right
ordinale ordinal
ordinato(a) tidy
orgoglioso(a) proud
orientale eastern
orizzontale horizontal
orrendo(a) awful
osceno(a) obscene
oscuro(a) unclear
ostile hostile
ostinato(a) stubborn
ottimista optimistic
ottimo(a) excellent
ovvio(a) obvious
pacifico(a) peaceful
pallido(a) pale
paralizzato(a) paralyzed
parecchi(e) quite a lot of
pari even
parziale partial
passato(a) last
passivo(a) passive
pauroso(a) awful
pazzo(a) crazy
pedonale pedestrian
peggiore worse
pelato(a) bald
peloso(a) hairy
pensieroso(a) thoughtful
penultimo(a) second from last
perfetto(a) perfect
pericoloso(a) dangerous
permaloso(a) touchy
permanente permanent
perplesso(a) puzzled
perso(a) lost
personale personal
perverso(a) perverse
pesante heavy
pessimista pessimistic
pessimo(a) very bad
piacevole pleasant
piatto(a) flat
piccante hot; spicy
piccolo(a) small; little; young
pieghevole folding
pieno(a) full
pignolo(a) fastidious

pigro(a) lazy
pittoresco(a) picturesque
poco(a) little
  pochi(e) few
popolare popular
portatile portable
potente powerful
povero(a) poor; unfortunate
pratico(a) practical
precipitoso(a) rash
preciso(a) precise
preferito(a) favourite
preoccupato(a) worried
presbite long-sighted
presuntuoso(a) conceited
prezioso(a) precious
primo(a) first
principale main
privato(a) private
profondo(a) deep
profumato(a) fragrant
pronto(a) ready
prossimo(a) next
provvisorio(a) provisional; temporary
prudente careful
pubblico(a) public
pudico(a) modest; demure
pulito(a) clean
puzzolente stinking
quadrato(a) square
qualche some
qual(e) which; what
qualsiasi any
quanto(a) how much
  quante(i) how many
quello(a) that
  quelli(e) those
questo(a) this
  questi(e) these
quotidiano(a) daily
radicale radical
raffinato(a) sophisticated
ragionevole sensible; reasonable
randagio(a) stray
rapido(a) quick
raro(a) rare
rauco(a) hoarse
reale true
recente recent
redditizio(a) profitable
regionale regional
regolare regular
resistente strong
responsabile responsible
rettangolare rectangular
ricamato(a) embroidered
ricaricabile rechargeable
riccio(a) curly
ricco(a) rich
riconoscente grateful
ricoperto(a) covered
ridicolo(a) funny
ridotto(a) reduced
riflessivo(a) reflexive
rigido(a) stiff
ripido(a) steep
ripieno(a) stuffed
rischioso(a) risky
riservato(a) reserved
risolto(a) solved
robusto(a) strong
roco(a) hoarse
rotondo(a) round
rotto(a) broken
rumoroso(a) noisy
ruvido(a) rough
sacro(a) sacred

saggio(a) wise
salato(a) salty
sano(a) healthy; sane
santo(a) holy
saporito(a) tasty
sbadato(a) careless
sbagliato(a) wrong
sbiadito(a) faded
sbronzo(a) drunk
scadente poor-quality
scalzo(a) barefoot
scarico(a) not loaded; flat
scarso(a) scarce
scemo(a) stupid
schifoso(a) disgusting
schizzinoso(a) fussy
sciocco(a) silly
scivoloso(a) slippery
scolastico(a) school
scollato(a) low-cut
scolorito(a) faded
scomodo(a) uncomfortable
sconosciuto(a) unknown
scontento(a) unhappy
sconvolto(a) upset
scoperto(a) bare; uncovered
scorretto(a) incorrect
scorrevole flowing; fluent
scorso(a) last
scortese rude; impolite
scosso(a) shaken
scotto(a) overcooked
scremato(a) skimmed
scuro(a) dark
seccato(a) annoyed
secco(a) dry
secondo(a) second
segreto(a) secret
seguente following
selvaggio(a) wild
selvatico(a) wild
semplice simple
sensibile sensitive
sensuale sensual
sentimentale sentimental
separato(a) separate; separated
serale evening
sereno(a) calm
serio(a) serious
sessuale sexual
settentrionale northern
settimanale weekly
severo(a) strict; severe
sfacciato(a) cheeky
sfinito(a) exhausted
sfocato(a) out of focus
sfortunato(a) unlucky
sgarbato(a) rude
sgonfio(a) flat
sgradevole unpleasant
sgraziato(a) clumsy
sicuro(a) safe
sieronegativo(a) HIV-negative
sieropositivo(a) HIV-positive
silenzioso(a) quiet
simile similar
simpatico(a) nice
sincero(a) honest
sinistro(a) left
sintetico(a) synthetic
sleale disloyal
snello(a) slim
snervante stressful
sobrio(a) sober
sociale social
socievole sociable
soddisfatto(a) pleased
soffice soft

soffocante stifling
sofisticato(a) sophisticated
solare solar; sun
solido(a) solid
solitario(a) lonely
solito(a) usual
solo(a) alone
sonoro(a) loud
soprannaturale supernatural
sordo(a) deaf
sordomuto(a) deaf-and-dumb
sorprendente surprising
sorpreso(a) surprised
sorridente smiling
sospettoso(a) suspicious
sotterraneo(a) underground
sottile thin
sottinteso(a) understood
sovraccarico(a) overloaded
spaesato(a) lost
spaventoso(a) terrible
spazioso(a) spacious
speciale special
spensierato(a) carefree
spento(a) off
spesso(a) thick
spettinato(a) uncombed
spezzato(a) broken
spiacevole unpleasant
spiritoso(a) witty
spontaneo(a) spontaneous
sporco(a) dirty
sposato(a) married
squallido(a) dingy
squilibrato(a) deranged
squisito(a) delicious
stabile stable
stagionato(a) seasoned
stanco(a) tired
stonato(a) tone-deaf
stordito(a) stunned
storico(a) historical; memorable
storto(a) crooked
stradale road
straniero(a) foreign
strano(a) strange
straordinario(a) extraordinary
stravagante eccentric
stravolto(a) distraught
stressante stressful
stressato(a) stressed
stretto(a) narrow; tight
stridulo(a) shrill
studioso(a) studious
stufo(a) fed up
stupendo(a) wonderful
subacqueo(a) underwater
successivo(a) following
sudato(a) sweaty
suo(a) his; her; your
superbo(a) proud; haughty
superfluo(a) superfluous
superiore upper; secondary
supplementare extra
surgelato(a) frozen
svantaggiato(a) disadvantaged
sveglio(a) awake
svelto(a) quick
tagliente sharp
tale such
tanto(a) a lot of
tascabile pocket-sized
tenero(a) tender
teso(a) tense
testardo(a) stubborn
tiepido(a) lukewarm
tipico(a) typical; traditional
tirchio(a) mean

tondo(a) round
tranquillo(a) quiet
triste sad
troppi(e) too many
troppo(a) too much
tuo(a) your
turbato(a) upset
tutto(a) all
ubriaco(a) drunk
ufficiale official
uguale equal
ultimo(a) last; latest
umano(a) human
umido(a) damp
umile humble
unico(a) only
unto(a) greasy
urgente urgent
usato(a) second-hand
utile useful
valido(a) valid
vario(a) varied; various
vecchio(a) old
vegetale vegetable
vegetariano(a) vegetarian
velenoso(a) poisonous
veloce fast
vergognoso(a) terrible
vero(a) true; real; genuine
vicino(a) near; close by
vietato(a) forbidden
vivace lively; bright
vivo(a) alive; live
viziato(a) spoilt
vostro(a) your
vuoto(a) empty
zitto(a) quiet
zoppo(a) lame
zuccherato(a) sweetened
zuppo(a) soaked; drenched

ADVERBS AND PREPOSITIONS

What is an adverb?
An **adverb** is a word usually used with verbs, adjectives or other adverbs that gives more information about when, how, where or in what cirumstances something happens, or to what degree something is true, for example, *quickly*, *happily*, *now*, *extremely*, *very*.

What is a preposition?
A **preposition** is a word such as *at*, *for*, *with*, *into* or *from*, which is usually followed by a noun, pronoun, or, in English, a word ending in *-ing*. Prepositions show how people or things relate to the rest of the sentence, for example, *She's at home*; *a tool for cutting grass*; *It's from David*.

a at; in; to
abbastanza quite; enough
accanto near
addirittura even
adesso now
affatto at all
allora then; so
almeno at least
altrettanto equally
altrimenti or; another way
ancora still; more; again
appena just; only just
apposta on purpose; specially
assai very; much
assieme together
attorno round
attraverso through
attualmente at the moment
avanti forward
  in avanti forward
bene well
ci there; here
cioè that is
circa about
come how; like; as
comunque anyway
con with
continuamente nonstop
contro against
correntemente fluently
così so; like this
da from; to; since
daccapo from the beginning
dappertutto everywhere
davanti at the front; in front of; opposite
davvero really
dentro in; inside
di of; by
dietro behind
diritto straight on
domani tomorrow
dopo after; later; then
dopodomani the day after tomorrow
doppio double
dove where
dovunque wherever; everywhere

durante during
eccetto except
ecco here
entro by
  entro domani by tomorrow
esattamente exactly
essenzialmente essentially
estremamente extremely
evidentemente obviously
fa ago
finalmente at last
fino a until; as far as
finora yet; so far
forse maybe
forte fast; hard; loud
fra between; among; in
  fra poco soon
fuori outside; out
già already
giù down
giusto just
gratis free
gravemente seriously
ieri yesterday
improvvisamente suddenly; unexpectedly
in in; to; into; by
incirca: all'incirca about
indietro back
infine finally
infuori out
innanzitutto first of all
inoltre besides
insieme together
insomma well
intanto for now; but
intorno round
inutilmente unnecessarily
invece but
  invece di instead of
là (over) there
laggiù down there; over there
lassù up there
lentamente slowly
lì there
liscio smoothly
lontano far
  da lontano from a distance
lungo along
mai never
  quasi mai hardly ever
  mai più never again
malapena: a malapena hardly
male badly
malgrado in spite of
mediante by means of
meglio better
meno less; fewer; minus; except
  a meno che unless
  di meno less
  più o meno more or less
  meno... di less... than
molto a lot; much; very
naturalmente of course
neanche not even; neither
  non ... neanche not even...
nemmeno not even; neither
  non ... nemmeno not even...
no no; not
non not
nonostante in spite of
nuovamente again
oggi today
oggigiorno nowadays
oltre over
  oltre a apart from
ora now; **per ora** for now
ormai by now

ovunque wherever; everywhere
peggio worse
per for; through; by; to
perché why
perfettamente perfectly
perfino even
persino even
piano slowly; quietly
  pian piano little by little
più more
  più di more than
  di più more
  in più more
  più o meno more or less
  mai più never again
piuttosto rather
po': un po' a little
poco not much
  tra poco soon
poi then; later
  prima o poi sooner or later
praticamente practically
precisamente precisely
pressappoco about
presto soon; early
prima before; earlier
  prima possibile as soon as possible
principalmente mainly
proprio just; really
purtroppo unfortunately
qua (over) here
quaggiù down here
quando when
quanto how much; how long
quasi nearly; hardly
  quasi mai hardly ever
quassù up here
qui here
quindi then
rapidamente quickly
raramente rarely
realmente really
recentemente recently
salvo except
secondo according to
sempre always; still
  per sempre forever
  sempre meno less and less
senza without
sì yes
solamente only
solo only
soltanto only
sopra over; above; on top of
  di sopra upstairs
soprattutto mainly; especially
sotto under; below
sottosopra upside down
sottoterra underground
sottovoce in a low voice; softly
specialmente especially
spesso often
stamattina this morning
stanotte tonight; last night
stasera this evening
stavolta this time
su on; up; about
subito immediately
talmente so much; so
tanto so; so much
tardi late
tra between; among; in
tranne except
troppo too
tuttavia but
ultimamente lately
veramente really; actually

verso towards; about *(of time)*
vi there
via away
viceversa vice versa
volentieri willingly

SOME EXTRA NOUNS

> **What is a noun?**
> A noun is a naming word for a living being, a thing, or an idea, for example, *woman*, *Andrew*, *desk*, *happiness*.

l' **abbazia** abbey
l' **abbigliamento** clothes
l' **abbreviazione** *f* abbreviation
l' **abilità** skill
l' **abitante** *m/f* inhabitant
l' **abitudine** *f* habit
l' **aborto** abortion; miscarriage
l' **accento** accent; stress
l' **accesso** access
l' **accordo** agreement; chord
l' **addestramento** training
l' **addizione** *f* sum
l' **affermazione** *f* statement
l' **affetto** affection
l' **aggettivo** adjective
l' **aiuto** help
l' **alfabeto** alphabet
l' **alimentazione** *f* diet
l' **alito** breath
l' **allarme** *m* alarm
l' **allenamento** training
l' **allenatore** *m* coach
l' **allenatrice** *f* coach
l' **alloggio** accommodation
l' **allusione** *f* hint
l' **alternativa** alternative
l' **ambiente** *m* environment
l' **ambizione** *f* ambition
l' **amicizia** friendship
l' **ammirazione** *f* admiration
l' **amore** *m* love
l' **analfabeta** *m/f* illiterate
l' **analgesico** painkiller
l' **anestesia** anaesthesia
l' **angelo** angel
l' **angolo** corner; angle
l' **anima** soul
l' **anticipo** advance
essere in anticipo to be early
l' **antifurto** *(pl inv)* burglar alarm; car alarm
l' **apertura** opening
l' **apostrofo** apostrophe
l' **apparecchio** device; brace
l' **appoggio** support
l' **apprendimento** learning
l' **argomento** subject
l' **ascella** armpit
l' **aspetto** appearance
l' **assenza** absence
l' **assicurazione** *f* insurance
l' **associazione** *f* association
l' **astuccio** case
l' **atmosfera** atmosphere
l' **atrio** entrance; concourse
l' **attaccapanni** *m (pl inv)* hook
l' **atteggiamento** attitude
l' **attentato** attack
l' **attenzione** *f* attention
l' **attesa** wait
l' **attimo** minute
l' **attività** *(pl inv)* activity
l' **attualità** current affairs
l' **audizione** *f* audition
l' **aumento** increase
l' **autografo** autograph

l' autorità *(pl inv)* authority
l' avorio ivory
l' avvenimento event
l' avventura adventure; affair
l' azione *f* action; deed; share
la bacinella bowl
la badante care worker
la bancarella stall
la banconota note
la bandiera flag
la bara coffin
la baracca *(pl* **-che***)* hut
il barattolo jar; tin; pot
il barboncino poodle
il barbone tramp
la barella stretcher
la barzelletta joke
la battuta jok
il becco (*pl* **-chi**) beak
la beneficenza charity
la bevanda drink
la biancheria sheets and towels; underwear
la bilancia *(pl* **-ce***)* scales
il bisogno need
il bivio junction
il/la blogger blogger
la bolletta bill
il bollitore kettle
la bombola cylinder
il bordo edge; border
  a bordo on board
il borotalco talcum powder
la briciola crumb
il brillante diamond
il brindisi toast
la buccia *(pl* **-ce***)* peel; rind
la bugia lie
la bugiarda liar
il bugiardo liar
il buonumore: essere di buonumore to be in a good mood
il burattino puppet
la bussola compass
la busta envelope
la bustarella bribe
la caccia hunting
il cacciatore hunter
il cadavere dead body
la caduta fall
la calamita magnet
il calcagno heel
la calligrafia handwriting
la calma calm
il calo drop
il camino chimney
il cammello camel
il campanile bell tower
il campionato championship
il cancello gate
la cannuccia *(pl* **-ce***)* drinking straw
il capitolo chapter
il capriccio whim
la capriola somersault
la caratteristica *(pl* **-che***)* feature
il carcere prison
la carestia famine
la cascata waterfall
la caserma barracks
il castigo *(pl* **-ghi***)* punishment
il catalogo *(pl* **-ghi***)* catalogue
la causa cause
la cenere ash
il cerchietto hairband
il cerchio circle
il cespuglio bush
la cicatrice scar
il cimitero graveyard

la circostanza circumstance
il citofono entry phone; intercom
il ciuccio dummy
la civiltà *(pl inv)* civilization
la classifica *(pl* **-che***)* results; charts; league table
il codino ponytail
il collasso collapse
il collegamento link
la colpa fault; blame
il/la colpevole culprit
il colpo blow; shot; raid
la combinazione combination; coincidence
la comitiva group
la commozione emotion
il/la complice accomplice
la complicità collusion
il computer fisso desktop computer
il/la concorrente competitor; contestant
la condizione condition
la confezione packet
la consegna delivery
la conseguenza consequence
il consiglio advice
la consolazione consolation
i contanti cash
il contenitore container
il contenuto contents
il continente continent; mainland
il conto bill; account; calculation
per conto mio in my opinion; on my own
il contrabbando smuggling
il contratto contract
la conversazione conversation
il coro choir
la correzione correction
la costruzione building
il crimine crime
la crisi *(pl inv)* crisis; fit
la croce cross
la crociera cruise
il cronometro stopwatch
il culturismo body-building
la cupola dome
la custodia case
il danno damage
il database *(pl inv)* database
il debito debt
la debolezza weakness
la decisione decision
il delitto crime
la delusione disappointment
la descrizione description
la destinazione destination
il dialetto dialect
la dichiarazione declaration; statement
la didascalia caption; subtitle
il difetto fault
la differenza difference
la diga (*pl* **-ghe**) dam; breakwater
il digiuno fasting
il/la dipendente employee
il dipinto painting
la disapprovazione disapproval
la discesa slope; descent
la disciplina discipline
il disco esterno *(pl* **-chi -i***)* external disk
il discorso speech
il disordine mess
il disprezzo contempt
la distruzione destruction
la dozzina dozen
l' eccezione *f* exception

l' eclisse *f* eclipse
l' entusiasmo enthusiasm
l' epoca *(pl* **-che***)* era
l' equitazione *f* riding
l' equivoco misunderstanding
l' eredità *(pl inv)* inheritance
l' esclamazione *f* exclamation
l' esempio example
l' esercito army
l' esilio exile
l' esperimento experiment
l' espressione *f* expression
l' estinzione *f* extinction
l' etichetta label
la faccenda matter
il fallimento bankruptcy; failure
la fantascienza science fiction
la fantasia imagination; pattern
il fare videogiochi gaming
il fascino charm
la fase phase
la fata fairy
la fatica *(pl* **-che***)* effort
il fatto fact
la felicità happiness
la ferita injury; wound
la fessura crack; slot
il fiato breath; stamina
il fidanzamento engagement
la fiducia trust
la filastrocca *(pl* **-che***)* nursery rhyme
il filo thread; yarn; wire
la finanza finance
il fine end
  fine settimana weekend
la fine end
  alla fine in the end
la firma signature
il fischio whistle
la fodera lining; cover
la fogna sewer
la folla crowd
la follia madness
la fortuna luck; fortune
la fototessera passport-size photo
la frattura fracture
la freccia *(pl* **-ce***)* arrow; indicator
il fumetto comic strip; comic
la funivia cablecar
la funzione function
la gabbia cage
la galera prison
il gambo stem
il gancio hook
la gara competition
la gelosia jealousy
la generazione generation
il genere kind; gender
il gesso chalk; plaster
la gestione management
il gettone token
il gioco per il computer computer game
la giornata day
la giostra roundabout
  le giostre funfair
la gita trip
il giudizio opinion
la giustificazione excuse
la goccia *(pl* **-ce***)* drop
il gonfiore swelling
il granello grain; speck
la gravidanza pregnancy
la gruccia *(pl* **-ce***)* crutch; coat hanger
il guasto failure
la guerra war

l' identità *(pl inv)* identity
l' illusione *f* illusion
l' imballaggio packing
l' immaginazione *f* imagination
l' impegno engagement; commitment
l' impianto system
l' importo amount
l' imposta shutter; tax
l' imprenditore *m* entrepreneur
l' imprenditrice *f* entrepreneur
l' impresa business
l' incertezza uncertainty
l' incubo nightmare
l' incursione *f* raid
l' indagine *f* investigation
l' indovinello riddle
l' inesperienza inexperience
l' inferno hell
l' infezione *f* infection
l' ingrediente *m* ingredient
l' iniezione *f* injection
l' inizio beginning
l' insegnamento teaching
l' intimità privacy
l' inviata correspondent
l' inviato correspondent
l' invidia envy
l' iscrizione *f* registration
il labbro lip
la lama blade
il lampadario chandelier
il lampo flash of lightning
la larghezza width
la lastra slab; sheet; X-ray
il lato side; aspect
la letteratura literature
il lettore DVD DVD player
il lievito yeast
la lineetta hyphen; dash
la lisca *(pl* **-che***)* fishbone
il livido bruise
la lotta struggle
la lunghezza length
il luogo *(pl* **-ghi***)* place
la macchia stain
la madrelingua mother tongue
la maga (*pl* **-ghe**) sorceress
il magazzino warehouse
la maggioranza majority
il/la maggiore the older; the oldest
la magia magic
il male evil
la maledizione curse
la maleducazione bad manners
la malinconia melancholy
il malinteso misunderstanding
la mancanza lack
la manciata handful
le manette handcuffs
la manifestazione demonstration; event
la maniglia handle
la maratona marathon
la marca *(pl* **-che***)* make; brand
il masterizzatore DVD DVD writer
il mazzo bunch; pack
la media average
il/la mendicante beggar
la mensola shelf
la mente mind
la menzogna lie
la merce goods
il mestiere job
la metà *(pl inv)* half
il miglioramento improvement
la minaccia *(pl* **-ce***)* threat
la minoranza minority

il miracolo miracle
la miseria poverty
il mito myth
la mitologia mythology
il/la mittente sender
la modifica *(pl* **-che***)* modification; alteration
il modulo form
la morte death
la mostra exhibition
il motivo reason
la multa fine
il mutuo mortgage
il nascondiglio hiding place
il nastro ribbon; tape
il navigatore internet internet user
la nazione nation
il neo mole
la neonata newborn baby
il neonato newborn baby
il nodo knot; tangle
la noia boredom
la norma norm
la nostalgia homesickness
le nozze wedding
l' obbligo *(pl* **-ghi***)* obligation
l' obiettivo lens; aim
l' obiezione *f* objection
l' occasione *f* opportunity; occasion; bargain
l' odio hatred
l' odore *m* smell
l' offesa insult
l' omaggio gift
l' ombelico (*pl* **-chi**) navel
l' omicidio murder
l' onestà honesty
l' opinione *f* opinion
l' opuscolo booklet
l' organizzazione *f* organization
l' origine *f* origin
l' orizzonte *m* horizon
l' orlo edge; brink; brim; hem
l' orma track; footprint
l' ormone *m* hormone
l' ortografia spelling
l' osservazione *f* observation; remark
l' ossigeno oxygen
l' ostacolo difficulty; hurdle
l' ostaggio hostage
l' ottimismo optimism
l' otturazione *f* filling
il paesaggio landscape
la palestra gym
la palude marsh
il pannello panel
il panno cloth
il paracadute *(pl inv)* parachute
il paradiso heaven
il paragrafo paragraph
il pareggio draw
la parentesi *(pl inv)* bracket
il parere *m* opinion
la parolaccia *(pl* **-ce***)* swearword
il particolare detail
il/la passante passer-by
il passatempo pastime
il passato past
la passione passion
il pasto meal
il patto pact
la pazza madman
il pazzo madman
il peccato shame; sin
il pedaggio toll
il pedone pedestrian
il/la pendolare commuter

il pennello paintbrush
il pensiero thought; worry
la pensionata pensioner
il pensionato pensioner
la percentuale percentage
il percorso route
la perdita loss; waste
la permanenza stay
il personaggio character
il personale staff
la personalità *(pl inv)* personality
la peste plague; pest
la pettinatura hairstyle
il pettine comb
il pianerottolo landing
il pianeta planet
il piatto dish; plate; **i piatti** the cymbals
la piega (*pl* **-ghe**) fold; pleat; crease
la pietà pity
la pigrizia laziness
la pinacoteca *(pl* **-che***)* art gallery
il pisolino nap
la pistola gun
la piuma feather
il pizzico (*pl* **-chi**) pinch
il podio podium
la polemica *(pl* **-che***)* controversy
il polline pollen
la pomata ointment
la popolazione population
il popolo people
il portatelefonino mobile phone case
il/la portavoce *(pl inv)* spokesperson
il portone main entrance
la porzione portion
la posa exposure; pose
le posate cutlery
la posizione position
la possibilità *(pl inv)* possibility; opportunity
il post *(pl inv)* post (*on forum or blog*)
la potenza power
il potere power
la povertà poverty
la precauzione precaution
la preda prey
la prefazione preface
la preferenza preference
la preghiera prayer
il pregio good quality
il pregiudizio prejudice
il prelievo withdrawal
la premiazione prize-giving; award ceremony
la preoccupazione worry
i preparativi preparations
la presa grip
il presepio crib
il preservativo condom
la pressione pressure
il prestito loan
il preventivo estimate
il/la principiante beginner
il principio beginning; principle
la probabilità *(pl inv)* chance
il problema problem
la profondità depth
il progetto plan
il progresso progress
il proiettile bullet
la prolunga (*pl* **-ghe**) extension
il pronome pronoun
la pronuncia *(pl* **-ce***)* pronunciation
il proposito intention
la proposizione clause

la proposta suggestion
la prospettiva prospect; perspective
la protezione protection
la provetta test tube
il provino screen test; trailer
la provocazione provocation
il provvedimento measure
il pubblico public; audience
la punizione punishment
la punta point; top; touch
doppie punte split ends
la puntata episode; flying visit
la punteggiatura punctuation
il punteggio score
il punto point; stitch; full stop
la puntura injection; sting; bite
la puzza stink
il quadrifoglio four-leaf clover
la questione matter
la quota membership fee
il quotidiano daily paper
la raccolta collection
il raccolto harvest
il racconto short story
la radiazione radiation
la radice root
la ragione reason
il ramo branch; field
il rapimento kidnapping
la rapina robbery
il rapporto relationship; report
la rappresentazione representation; play
la rata instalment
la razza race; breed; sort
il razzismo racism
il reato crime
la reazione reaction
il rebus picture puzzle
la recensione review
il recipiente container
il reddito income
il regolamento rules
la reputazione reputation
il requisito requirement
la respirazione breathing
il respiro breath
la riabilitazione rehabilitation
il riassunto summary
il ricatto blackmail
il ricciolo curl
la ricerca (*pl* **-che**) search; research; project
la richiesta request
la ricompensa reward
la ricreazione recreation; break
il riferimento reference
il rifiuto refusal
la riflessione remark; thought
il riflesso reflection; reflex
il rimorso remorse
il rimpianto regret
il Rinascimento Renaissance
la ringhiera railing; banisters
il rinvio (*pl* **-ii**) postponement
il risparmio saving
il rispetto respect
la risposta answer
il ritornello refrain
il ritratto portrait
la rivelazione revelation
la rivincita rematch
la ruga (*pl* **-ghe**) wrinkle
la ruggine rust
la rugiada dew
il sacrificio sacrifice
la sagoma outline; shape

la salita climb; hill
il salvadanaio money box
lo sbadiglio yawn
lo sbaglio mistake
la sbarra bar
la scadenza expiry date; sell-by date; use-by date
lo scaffale bookcase
lo scatto click; spurt
la scelta choice
lo sceneggiato TV drama
lo scheletro skeleton
lo schema diagram
lo scherzo joke
la schiava slave
lo schiavo slave
la schiuma foam; lather
lo schizzo splash; sketch
la sciagura disaster
lo scioglilingua *(pl inv)* tongue-twister
la scommessa bet
la sconfitta defeat
lo sconto discount
lo scontrino receipt slip
lo scontro crash; clash
la scoperta discovery
lo scopo aim
lo scoppio explosion; bang
la scorciatoia short cut
la scottatura burn; sunburn
la scrittura writing
la scrivania desk
lo scudo shield
la scusa excuse
la seccatura nuisance; bother
la semifinale semifinal
la sensazione feeling
il senso sense; direction
il settore sector
la sezione section
la sfida challenge
lo sfondo background
la sfortuna bad luck
lo sforzo effort
lo sfruttamento exploitation
la sfumatura shade; tone
lo sgabello stool
lo sgabuzzino junk room
lo sguardo look
la siccità drought
la sicurezza safety
la sigla acronym
il significato meaning
il silenzio silence
la sillaba syllable
il simbolo symbol
il sinonimo synonym
il sintomo symptom
il sistema system; way
la sistemazione accommodation
la situazione situation
lo smacchiatore stain remover
la smagliatura ladder; stretch mark
la soddisfazione satisfaction
il soffio breath
il solitario game of patience
la solitudine loneliness
il sollievo relief
la soluzione solution
il sommario summary
la sonnambula sleepwalker
il sonnambulo sleepwalker
il sonnifero sleeping pill
il sonno sleep
il soprannome nickname
il sorso sip
la sorte fate

il/la sosia *(pl inv)* double
il sospetto suspicion
il sospiro sigh
il sostantivo noun
la sostituzione substitution
la sovvenzione subsidy
la spaccatura split
la spacciatrice drug dealer
lo spacciatore drug dealer
lo spacco (*pl* **-chi**) slit
lo spago *(pl* **-ghi***)* string
la spallina shoulder strap
lo sparo shot
lo spavento fright
lo specchietto pocket mirror
la specialità *(pl inv)* speciality
la specie *(pl inv)* sort; species
la speculazione speculation
la speranza hope
lo spettatore viewer; spectator
gli spettotori the audience
le spezie spices
la spia spy; light
gli spiccioli loose change
lo spiedino kebab; skewer
la spiegazione explanation
la spinta push
lo sportello door; window
lo spuntino snack
lo starnuto sneeze
la stenografia shorthand
la stilografica *(pl* **-che***)* fountain pen
la stima respect
la strage massacre
lo straordinario overtime
lo strappo tear; lift
lo strato layer
la strega (*pl* **-ghe**) witch
lo strillo scream
la striscia (*pl* **-sce**) strip
lo striscione banner
la struttura structure
lo stupore amazement
lo stupro rape
il suggerimento suggestion
il suicidio suicide
la suoneria alarm; ringtone
il suono sound
la superficie surface
il/la superiore superior
la superstizione superstition
lo svantaggio disadvantage
il taglio cut
la tappa stop
la targa (*pl* **-ghe**) number plate
la targhetta nameplate; name tag
la tastiera keyboard
il tasto key (*on keyboard*)
il tatuaggio tattoo
la teiera teapot
la tela cloth
il temperino penknife
la tentazione temptation
la teoria theory
il terreno land; ground
il territorio territory
il/la terrorista terrorist
il teschio skull
il tessuto fabric
il testamento will
il/la testimone witness
la tifosa supporter
il tifoso supporter
il tipo sort; type
la tomba grave
il tono tone
il torcicollo stiff neck
il tornante hairpin bend

il torneo tournament
il totocalcio the pools
la traccia *(pl* **-ce***)* trace
la tradizione tradition
la traduzione translation
la trama plot
il tramonto sunset
il trapano drill
il trapianto transplant
il trasloco (*pl* **-chi**) removal
la trasmissione programme
il trattino hyphen
il tratto stretch
il trauma shock
la treccia *(pl* **-ce***)* plait
il tribunale court
il triciclo tricycle
il trono throne
il truffatore swindler
il tumore tumour
il tuorlo yolk
il turbante turban
l' udito hearing
l' umore *m* mood
l' unificazione *f* unification
l' urlo scream
l' usanza custom
il username *(pl inv)* username
l' uso use; usage
l' ustione *f* burn
la valanga (*pl* **-ghe**) avalanche
la valvola valve
il valzer *(pl inv)* waltz
il vandalismo vandalism
il vangelo gospel
la varietà variety
il vasetto jar
il vassoio tray
la vedova widow
il vedovo widower
il veicolo vehicle
il veleno poison
la vergogna embarrassment
la vernice varnish; paint; patent leather
la verità *(pl inv)* truth
il vero truth
la vicenda event; story
il vincitore winner
la vincitrice winner
la virgola comma; point
le virgolette inverted commas
la vita life; waist
la vittima victim
la vittoria victory
il vizio bad habit; vice
il vocabolario dictionary
il volo flight
la volontà will
il volume volume
il voto mark; vote
il vuoto gap
il wafer *(pl inv)* wafer
il water *(pl inv)* toilet
il W.C. *(pl inv)* W.C.
la zingara gypsy
lo zingaro gypsy
la zitella spinster
lo zoccolo clog; hoof; skirting board
lo zodiaco zodiac

VERBS

> **What is a verb?**
> A **verb** is a 'doing' word which describes what someone or something does, what someone or something is, or what happens to them, for example, *be*, *sing*, *live*.

abbandonare to abandon; to give up
abbassare to lower
abbracciarsi to hug
abbronzarsi to get tanned
abitare to live
abituarsi: abituarsi a (fare) qc to get used to (doing) sth
accadere to happen
accamparsi to camp
accarezzare to stroke
accelerare to accelerate
accendere to light; to turn on
accettare to accept
accludere to enclose
accogliere to welcome
accomodarsi to sit down
accompagnare to take ... to
accontentare to please
  accontentarsi di to make do with
accorciare to shorten
accorgersi to notice; to realize
acquistare to buy
addormentarsi to go/fall to sleep
adottare to adopt
afferrare to grab; to catch
affettare to slice
affittare to rent
affogare to drown
affondare to sink
affrettarsi to hurry up
agganciare to hook; to hang up
aggiungere to add
aggiustare to mend; to straighten
aggredire to attack
agire to act
agitare to shake
  agitarsi to worry
aiutare to help
allacciare to fasten; to connect
allagare to flood
allargare to widen
allearsi to join forces
allegare to enclose
allenare to train
alloggiare to stay
allungare to lengthen
alzare to lift; to raise
  alzarsi to get up
amare to love
ammalarsi to get ill
ammazzare to kill
ammettere to admit
ammirare to admire
andare to go
  andarsene to leave
annaffiare to water
annegare to drown
annoiare to bore
  annoiarsi to get bored
annullare to cancel
annunciare to announce
apparire to appear
appartenere to belong

appendere to hang
appoggiare to put; to lean
approfittare: approfittare di qc to make the most of sth
aprire to open; to turn on
arrabbiarsi to get angry
arrampicarsi to climb
arrangiarsi to get by
arrestare to arrest
arrivare to arrive
arrossire to blush
asciugare to dry
ascoltare to listen to
aspettare to wait; to expect
assaggiare to taste
assicurare to insure; to assure
assistere to look after; to watch; to witness
assomigliare a to look like
assumere to take on
atterrare to land
attirare to attract; to appeal to
attraversare to cross; to go through
aumentare to go up
avanzare to be left over
avere to have
  avere fame to be hungry
  avere sete to be thirsty
  avere paura to be afraid
  avere sonno to be sleepy
avvelenare to poison
avvertire to warn
avvicinare to move closer
baciare to kiss
badare to pay attention; to mind
bagnare to get wet; to water
ballare to dance
bastare to be enough
battere to beat; to hit
bere to drink
bestemmiare to swear
bisbigliare to whisper
bisticciare to quarrel
brillare to shine
brontolare to moan
bruciare to burn
bucare to have a puncture
  bucarsi to be on heroin
bussare to knock
buttare to throw
  buttare via to throw away
cacciare to hunt
cadere to fall
calare to decrease; to drop
calcolare to work out
cambiare to change
  cambiarsi to get changed
camminare to walk
cancellare to cancel; to delete
cantare to sing
capire to understand
  capire male to misunderstand
capitare to happen
caricare to (up)load; to charge
cavalcare to ride
cenare to have dinner
cercare to look for; to look up; to try
chiacchierare to chat
chiamare to call; to phone
chiarire to clarify
chiedere to ask; to ask for
  chiedersi to wonder
chiudere to close; to turn off
  chiudere a chiave to lock
cogliere to pick
coinvolgere to involve
collegare to connect
colpire to hit

comandare to be in charge
combattere to fight
cominciare to start
compilare to fill in
comporre to dial; to compose
comportarsi to behave
comprare to buy
condire to dress; to season
condividere to share
confermare to confirm
confondere to mix up
  confondersi to get mixed up
connettere to connect
conoscere to know
  conoscersi to meet
consegnare to deliver
conservare to keep
consigliare to recommend; to advise
consumare to wear out; to use
contare to count
  contare su qn to count on sb
contenere to contain
continuare to carry on
controllare to check
  controllarsi to control oneself
convenire to be cheaper
convincere to convince
  convincere qn a fare qc to persuade sb to do sth
copiare to copy
coprire to cover
correggere to correct; to mark
correre to run
costare to cost
credere to believe; to think
crescere to grow
cucinare to cook
cucire to sew
curare to treat
danneggiare to damage
dare to give
  dare su to look onto
decidere to decide
  decidersi to decide
decollare to take off
deludere to disappoint
denunciare to report; to expose
derubare to rob
descrivere to describe
desiderare to want
detrarre to deduct
deviare to divert
dichiarare to declare; to state
digerire to digest
dimagrire to lose weight
dimenticare to forget
dimettersi to resign
diminuire to decrease; to reduce
dimostrare to demonstrate
dipingere to paint
dire to say
dirigere to manage
discutere to discuss; to argue
disdire to cancel
disegnare to draw; to design
disfare to undo
distendere to stretch
  distendersi to lie down; to relax
distrarre to distract
  distrarsi to take one's mind off things
distribuire to distribute
distruggere to destroy
disubbidire: disubbidire a qn to disobey sb
diventare to become
divertire to amuse

divertirsi to have a good time
divorziare to get divorced
domandare to ask
domandarsi to wonder
dondolarsi to rock; to swing
dormire to sleep
dovere to have to
dovere qc a qn to owe sb sth
durare to last
emozionare: emozionarsi to be moved; to be excited
entrare to enter
esagerare to exaggerate
esaurire to sell out; to run out of
eseguire to carry out; to perform
esercitare to practise; to train
esigere to demand
esporre to display; to exhibit
esportare to export
esprimere to express
essere to be
estrarre to extract
evadere to escape
evitare to avoid
fabbricare to make
fallire to go bankrupt; to fail
fare to make; to do
fasciare to bandage
ferire to injure; to wound
fermare to stop
festeggiare to celebrate
fidanzarsi to get engaged
fidarsi: fidarsi di qn to trust sb
fingere to pretend
finire to finish
firmare to sign
fischiare to whistle
fissare to fix; to stare at
fornire to supply
forzare to force
fraintendere to misunderstand
fregare to pinch; to rub
frenare to brake
frequentare to go to; to see
friggere to fry
fuggire to escape
fumare to smoke
funzionare to work
galleggiare to float
garantire to guarantee
gelare to freeze
gestire to manage
gettare to throw
giocare to play
girare to turn
giudicare to judge
giurare to swear
gocciolare to drip
gonfiare to inflate
gonfiarsi to swell
graffiare to scratch
gridare to shout
guadagnare to earn; to gain
guardare to look at; to watch
guarire to cure; to heal up
guastarsi to break down
guidare to drive; to lead
ignorare to ignore
illudersi to deceive oneself
imbiancare to whitewash; to paint
imbrogliare to cheat
imbucare to post
immaginare to imagine; to think
impallidire to go pale
imparare to learn
impazzire to go mad
impedire: impedire a qn di fare qc to stop sb doing sth

impegnarsi: impegnarsi a fare qc to try hard to do sth
impiccarsi to hang oneself
importare to matter; to import
incartare to wrap
incassare to cash
incazzarsi to get pissed off
incendiare to set fire to
inciampare to trip
incominciare to start
incontrare to meet
incoraggiare to encourage
indagare: indagare su to investigate
indebolirsi to get weak
indicare to show; to point to
indirizzare to address; to send
indossare to wear
indovinare to guess
informare:informarsi su qc to ask about sth
ingannare to deceive
  ingannarsi to be mistaken
ingelosire to make jealous
ingessare to put in plaster
inghiottire to swallow
ingrandire to enlarge; to extend
ingrassare to make fat
  ingrassarsi to put on weight
iniziare to start
innaffiare to water
innamorarsi to fall in love
inquinare to pollute
insegnare to teach
inserire to insert
intasarsi to be blocked
intendere to mean
interrompere to interrupt
intervistare to interview
intitolare to name
  intitolarsi to be called
introdurre to introduce; to insert
invecchiare to get old
investire to run over; to invest
inviare to send
invidiare to envy
invitare to invite
iscriversi to register; to enrol; to join
lamentarsi to complain
lanciare to throw; to launch
lasciare to leave
  lasciarsi to split up
laurearsi to graduate
lavare to wash
  lavarsi i denti to brush one's teeth
lavorare to work
legare to tie
leggere to read
levare to take off
liberare to set free
  liberarsi to get away
licenziare to sack; to make redundant
  licenziarsi to give up one's job
litigare to quarrel
lottare to fight
lucidare to polish
maledire to curse
maltrattare to ill-treat
mancare to be missing; to be lacking
mandare to send
mangiare to eat
marcire to go rotten
masticare to chew
mentire to lie
meravigliarsi to be surprised
mescolare to mix
mettere to put

migliorare to improve
minacciare to threaten
misurare to measure
molestare to torment; to sexually harass
montare to assemble; to whip up
mordere to bite
morire to die
morsicare to bite
mostrare to show
muovere to move
nascere to be born
nascondere to hide
navigare to sail
  navigare in Internet to surf the Internet
negare to deny
nevicare to snow
noleggiare to hire; to hire out
notare to notice
  farsi notare to draw attention to oneself
nuotare to swim
obbedire to obey
obbligare: obbligare qn a fare qc to make sb do sth
occupare to occupy
  occuparsi di qn to look after sb
odiare to hate
offendere to insult
  offendersi to take offence
offrire to offer
ordinare to order
osare to dare
osservare to observe; to notice
ottenere to get
pagare to pay
parcheggiare to park
pareggiare to draw
parlare to speak; to talk
partecipare to take part in
partire to leave
passare to pass; to call by
passeggiare to stroll
peggiorare to get worse
pendere to hang
pensare to think
  pensare a to think about
perdere to lose; to leak
  perdersi to get lost
perdonare to forgive
permettere to allow
pesare to weigh
  pesarsi to weigh oneself
pescare to fish
pettinare to comb
piacere: mi piace I like it
piangere to cry
piantare to plant; to dump
picchiare to hit; to knock
piegare to fold; to bend
piovere to rain
piovigginare to drizzle
pisciare to piss
pitturare to paint
pizzicare to pinch; to itch
poggiare to place; to put
porre to put; to place
portare to take; to carry; to wear
posare to put
posteggiare to park
potere can
pranzare to have lunch
precipitare to fall
preferire to prefer
pregare to pray
  pregare qn di fare qc to ask sb to do sth

prelevare to withdraw
premere to press
premiare to give a prize to
prendere to take; to get
prenotare to book
preoccupare: preoccuparsi to worry
preparare to prepare
prescrivere to prescribe
prestare to lend
prestare attenzione to pay attention
prevedere to foresee; to plan for
procedere to get on
produrre to produce
progettare to plan
proibire to forbid
promettere to promise
proporre to suggest
proteggere to protect
provare to try; to try on; to feel; to prove
pubblicare to publish
pulire to clean
pungere to sting
punire to punish
puntare su to bet on
puzzare to stink
raccogliere to collect; to pick
raccomandare to recommend
raccontare to tell
raddrizzare to straighten
radere to shave
radersi to shave
raffreddare to cool
raffreddarsi to get cold
raggiungere to reach
ragionare to think
rallentare to slow down
rapinare to rob
rapire to kidnap
rappresentare to represent
rasare to shave off
rassicurare to reassure
reagire to react
realizzare to come true; to realize
recitare to act
recuperare to recover; to get back
regalare to give
reggere to hold
registrare to record
regnare to reign
regolare to adjust
remare to row
rendere to give back
rendersi conto di qc to realize sth
respirare to breathe
restare to stay; to remain
riaddormentarsi to go back to sleep
ricaricare to reload; to refill; to recharge
ricevere to receive
richiamare to call back
richiedere to ask for; to require
riciclare to recycle
ricominciare to start again
riconoscere to recognize
ricordare to remember
ricordare a qn di fare qc to remind sb to do sth
ridare to give… back
ridere to laugh
ridurre to reduce
riempire to fill (in)
rifare to do again
rifare il letto to make the bed
rifiutare to refuse
riguardare to concern; to consider

rilassarsi to relax
rimandare to put off
rimanere to stay; to remain
rimborsare to refund
rimettere to put back
  rimettersi to recover
rimpiangere to be sorry
rimproverare to tell off
rinchiudere to lock up
rinfrescare to freshen
  rinfrescarsi to freshen up
ringraziare to thank
rinnovare to renew
rintracciare to find
rinunciare to give up
rinviare to postpone
riparare to repair
  ripararsi da to shelter from
ripassare to come back; to revise
riposare to rest
riprendere: riprendersi to recover
riprovare to try again
riscaldare to warm up; to heat
rischiare to risk
risciacquare to rinse
riservare to book
risolvere to solve
risparmiare to save
rispettare to respect
rispondere to answer
ritirare to take out
ritornare to go back; to return
riuscire: riuscire a fare qc to succeed in doing sth
rivedere to see again
rompere to break
rotolare to roll
rovinare to ruin
rubare to steal
russare to snore
saldare to settle; to solder
salire to go up; to climb
  salire su to board
  salire in to get into
saltare to jump
salutare to say hello to; to say goodbye to
salvare to save; to rescue
sanguinare to bleed
sapere to know; to taste; to smell
sbadigliare to yawn
sbagliare to make a mistake
  sbagliarsi to be wrong
sbattere to slam
sbrigare to do
  sbrigarsi to hurry
sbucciare to peel; to shell
scadere to expire
scaldare to heat
scambiare to exchange
scappare to get away
scaricare to unload; to download
scartare to unwrap; to reject
scavare to dig
scegliere to choose
scendere to go down
  scendere da to get out of; to get off
scherzare to joke
schiacciare to squash
sciacquare to rinse
sciare to ski
scintillare to sparkle
sciogliere to dissolve; to undo
scivolare to slip; to slide
scommettere to bet
scomparire to disappear
sconfiggere to defeat

scongelare to defrost
sconsigliare to advise against
scontrarsi to clash; to run into
scopare to sweep
scoppiare to go off; to burst
scoprire to discover
scoraggiarsi to get discouraged
scottare to be hot
  scottarsi to get burnt
scrivere to write
scusare to excuse
  scusarsi to apologize
sdraiarsi to lie down
sedere to be sitting
  sedersi to sit
segnare to mark; to score
seguire to follow
selezionare to select
sembrare to look; to seem
sentire to hear; to feel
  sentirsi bene to feel well
  sentirsi male to feel ill
separare to separate
  separarsi to split up
seppellire to bury
servire to serve
  servire per qc to be for sth
sfidare to challenge
sfogliare to leaf through
sfuggire to escape
sgonfiare to deflate
sgridare: sgridare qn to tell sb off
significare to mean
singhiozzare to sob; to hiccup
sistemare to arrange; to settle
  sistemarsi to settle down; to find a job
slacciare to undo
slegare to untie
smarrire to lose
  smarrirsi to get lost
smettere to stop
smontare to take apart
soddisfare to satisfy
soffiare to blow
sognare to dream
somigliare: somigliare a to look like
sopportare to stand; to put up with
sorpassare to overtake
sorprendere to catch; to surprise
sorridere to smile
sorvegliare to watch
sospettare to suspect
sospirare to sigh
sostenere to support; to claim
sostituire to change
sottolineare to underline
sottovalutare to underestimate
sottrarre to subtract
spaccare to break
sparare to shoot
sparecchiare to clear the table
sparire to disappear
spaventare to scare
  spaventarsi to be scared
spedire to send
spegnere to put out; to turn off
spendere to spend
sperare to hope
spezzare to break
spiegare to explain
  spiegarsi to explain oneself
spingere to push; to drive
spogliare to undress
  spogliarsi to get undressed
spolverare to dust
sporcare to dirty

sposare to marry
sposarsi to get married
spostare to move
sprecare to waste
spremere to squeeze
sputare to spit
stabilire to fix
stabilirsi to settle
staccare to remove; to tear out
stampare to print
stancare: stancarsi to get tired
stare to be
stare fermo to keep still
stare zitto to be quiet
starnutire to sneeze
stendere to stretch; to hang out
stendersi to lie down
stirare to iron
stracciare to tear up
strappare to tear up
strillare to scream
stringere to be tight; to clasp
stufarsi: stufarsi di qc to get fed up with sth
subire to suffer; to undergo
succedere to happen
sudare to sweat
suicidarsi to commit suicide
suonare to play; to ring
superare to exceed; to overcome; to pass
supporre to suppose
svegliare: svegliarsi to wake up
svenire to faint
svestirsi to get undressed
sviluppare to develop
svitare to unscrew
svolgersi to happen
tacere to be quiet
tagliare to cut
tardare to be late
telefonare to phone
telefonare a qn to phone sb
tenere to hold; to keep
tentare to try
timbrare to stamp
tirare to pull; to throw
toccare to touch
togliere to take off; to take out
tornare to get back; to be back
tossire to cough
tradurre to translate
trascorrere to spend; to pass
trasferire to transfer
trasferirsi to move
traslocare to move
trasmettere to broadcast
trasportare to carry
trattare to treat
trattare di to be about
trattenere to hold back
tremare to shake
trovare to find
truccarsi to do one's make-up
tuffarsi to dive
ubriacarsi to get drunk
uccidere to kill
ungere to oil; to grease
unire to put together; to join
unirsi a to join
urlare to shout
usare to use
uscire to go out
utilizzare to use
valere to be worth
valere la pena to be worth it
valutare to value
vantarsi to boast

vedere to see
farsi vedere to be seen
vendere to sell
venire to come
vergognarsi to be ashamed; to be embarrassed
verificare to check
verificarsi to happen
verniciare to varnish; to paint
versare to pour; to spill; to pay in
vestirsi to get dressed
vestirsi da to dress up as
viaggiare to travel
vietare to forbid
vincere to win
violentare to rape
visitare to visit
vivere to live
volare to fly
volere to want
voler bene a qn to like sb; **voler dire** to mean
voltare to turn
votare to vote
vuotare to empty
zoppicare to limp

ENGLISH INDEX

The words on the following pages cover all of the ESSENTIAL and IMPORTANT NOUNS in the book.

English index